VERMEER

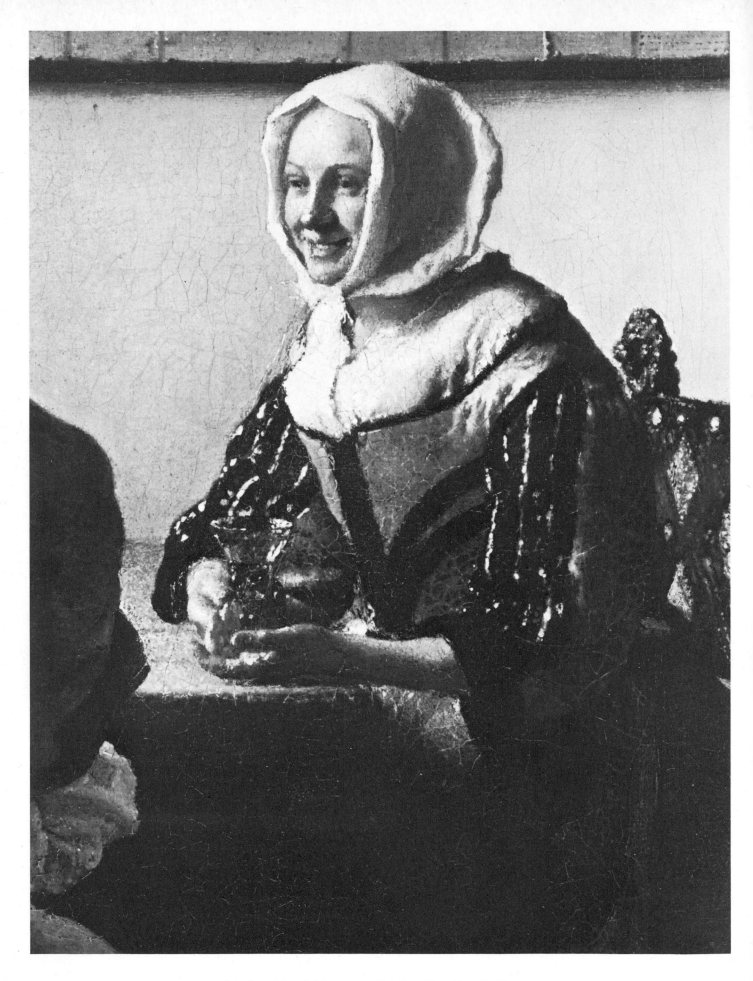

Interior with a Soldier and a Girl Laughing (detail) Plate 9

VERMEER

CHRISTOPHER WRIGHT

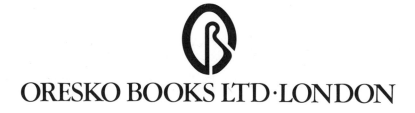

ORESKO BOOKS LTD·LONDON

ACKNOWLEDGEMENTS

The Music Lesson is reproduced by Gracious Permission of Her Majesty the Queen. I would like to thank the following for their help in kindly providing photographs and information: the marquess of Bath; Baron Rolin; Sir Alfred Beit; Service de Documentation Photographique de la Réunion des Musées Nationaux; Edition Joachim Blauel; Jörg P. Anders (Plates 10 and 24); Boymans van Beuningen Museum, Rotterdam; Courtauld Institute of Art, London; The Frick Collection, New York; Herzog Anton-Ulrich Museum, Brunswick; Institute of Arts, Detroit; Isabella Stewart Gardner Museum, Boston; Iveagh Bequest, Kenwood, London; Kunsthistorisches Museum, Vienna; Mauritshuis, The Hague; Metropolitan Museum of Art, New York; Musée du Louvre, Paris; Museum of Fine Arts, Boston; National Gallery, London; National Gallery of Scotland, Edinburgh; National Gallery of Art, Washington; Rijksmuseum, Amsterdam; Staatliche Gemäldegalerie, Berlin-Dahlem; Staatliche Gemäldegalerie, Dresden; Städelsches Kunstinstitut, Frankfurt-am-Main. Many other people have helped in various ways both great and small, in particular Jean Decoen, Dr. Franz Eggemann, Anne Hunter, Jacques Le Plus, M. and Mme. Pion, Keith Roberts, Kate de Rothschild and Spencer Samuels. I have had several profitable discussions with friends and colleagues, especially with David Wakefield. In addition Robert Oresko has been an impatient but encouraging taskmaster throughout the work on this book.

In Memoriam
VITALE BLOCH

First published in Great Britain by
Oresko Books Ltd., 30 Notting Hill Gate, London W11

ISBN 0 905368 00 2 (cloth)
ISBN 0 905368 04 5 (paper)
Copyright © Oresko Books Ltd. 1976

Printed in Great Britain by
Burgess and Son (Abingdon) Ltd., Abingdon, Oxfordshire

Contents

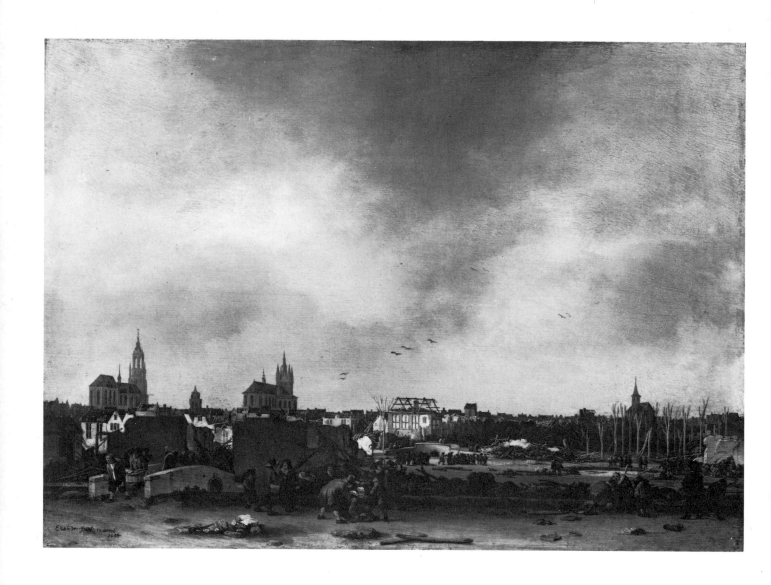

fig. 1 Egbert van der POEL
The Ruins of Delft after the Explosion of 1654
Panel 36.2 × 49.5 cm.
Signed and dated 1654
London, National Gallery

Many versions of this picture exist, thus
indicating the importance of the catastrophe
in the eyes of Vermeer's contemporaries. The
damage seems to have been confined to the
houses on one side of the town as both the
churches survived unscathed. Delft obviously
took some considerable time to recover as can
be seen by the partly overgrown ruins in the
picture by Daniel Vosmaer in the Johnson
Collection at Philadelphia. Vermeer depicted,
in *The View of Delft*, the side of the town
undamaged in the explosion.

Johannes Vermeer

ON 12 OCTOBER 1654 much of the prosperous town of Delft was destroyed by the explosion of a powder magazine. Many people died and among those killed was no less an artist than Carel Fabritius. He had been a pupil of Rembrandt and was already an established master in Delft, painting in an accomplished and highly individual style. Thus in 1667 van Bleyswyck was able to make his famous comment that Johannes Vermeer rose out of the ashes of the fire that had consumed Fabritius.

Vermeer was only twenty-two at the time of the explosion which must have done serious damage to the artistic tradition of the town. The physical extent of the disaster is recorded in a picture by Egbert van der Poel in the National Gallery, London (fig. 1). The young Vermeer, therefore, began his career under unusual circumstances which could serve as a partial explanation for his obscure and eclectic early pictures.

It is often accepted with reluctance that most of the important painters of the seventeenth century began their careers working in a seemingly uncharacteristic idiom. This is true even of the relatively stable Dutch society of the time. Rembrandt's earliest pictures make little sense when seen in isolation, and Vermeer was no exception to this pattern. He began his career imitating not the traditions of his home town, and not even Carel Fabritius, as most writers would have it, but by the incomplete assimilation of the Caravaggesque masters of the Catholic city of Utrecht. It is almost tempting to think that Vermeer spent some time there in his youth, but this need not have been so as he certainly owned an important picture by the Utrecht artist Dirck van Baburen (fig. 11) which appears in the background of two of his pictures. Vermeer was an art dealer and connoisseur and, if the backgrounds of his paintings are taken as evidence, he owned many different kinds of pictures which included seascapes and landscapes as well as religious and mythological works.

What is most difficult to undertake is the reconstruction of Vermeer's career in Delft in the early 1650s. Such a reconstruction has been attempted once, by van Meegeren who was daring enough to fill a gap in Vermeer's life by producing what purported to be the artist's first faltering and obviously eclectic pictures. There are now two serious candidates for this dubious period but even today the memory of van Meegeren is

too fresh for newly discovered pictures to be accepted without hesitation into the canon of Vermeer's early works.

The first is the astonishing picture of *Esther before Ahasuerus* (fig. 2) in the collection of Jean Decoen at Knokke-Zoute. Signed and dated 1654 the picture is on an enormous scale with several life-size figures. Most of the figures in the background seem to be derived from the art of Hendrick Terbrugghen, and, thus, are accomplished in a derivative sort of way. The main figures, however, are far more original and are quite unlike anything else painted at the time. The colours are extravagant, even confused, and, although sceptics who have not seen the picture may wonder how this unlikely object could have been created by the master of Delft, there are many points which look forward to surer ground. The face and drapery of the helmeted soldier on the left are reminiscent in handling of the Edinburgh *Christ in the House of Martha and Mary* (Plate 1), while the still life on the carpet-covered table, which strikes an incongruous note in this picture, was to become one of Vermeer's favourite interests. The dog lost in shadow is rather like the improbable animal in The Hague *Diana and her Companions* (Plate 2). All these similarities cannot prove that Vermeer painted the *Esther* but they point at least to the fact that the picture deserves serious consideration as his earliest surviving work.

Even more remote from the Vermeer we know is the *St. Praxedis* (fig. 3) of 1655, which is with Spencer Samuels Inc. in New York. The saint is seen squeezing the sponge with which she has mopped up the blood of the Christian martyrs. Vermeer's signature and date are convincing from the scientific point of view as they have been examined in a laboratory, but the picture itself is a copy of one painted by the obscure seventeenth century Florentine artist Felice Ficherelli. If it were not for the fact that Vermeer is documented as an expert in Italian painting there would hardly be a historical reason for attributing this picture to him at all. Yet in the intense colour and rich, almost juicy handling of the paint there is a clear similarity with the much damaged *Diana and her Companions* at The Hague.

Vermeer's other two early pictures, both of which are or were signed, have been in the picture galleries of Edinburgh and The Hague long enough for their improbability to be accepted. The Edinburgh *Christ in the House of Martha and Mary* could be interpreted as an unsuccessful but striking essay in the manner of Terbrugghen, painted when the work of this master, who died in 1629, had gone out of fashion.

The three figures are large and almost fill the picture plane, but Vermeer was not quite able to relate them to each other. Mary, positioned nearest to the spectator, seems to lean uneasily out of the picture. The paint is handled broadly but with less assurance than Terbrugghen. The *Diana* is at first sight more unified in composition, yet, again, the integration of the figures with the landscape background is uncertain and tentative.

All the pictures so far discussed have at some point been doubted and they will continue to be so. Vermeer's early career will remain for ever a ground for speculation unless more evidence turns up. Indeed the first picture by Vermeer of which we can be absolutely certain is the Dresden *Procuress* (Plate 3). Signed and dated 1656, it forms a concrete point of departure from the first four pictures about which so many uncertainties exist, towards the moment when he became an artist unique in his time. No one can tell how long this process took, and, although many attempts have been made to propose a precise chronology, there is no evidence. The pictures can be put into approximate groupings according to subject matter and style, but their precise order remains elusive. It seems reasonable, however, to suppose that if Vermeer was painting pictures in the style of *The Procuress* at the age of twenty-four, it is a near certainty that he needed several more years to acquire the experience necessary to paint the celebrated *View of Delft* (Plate 5).

The Procuress is a noisy picture, full of impasto, bright colour and lascivious intent. Vermeer did not try, as he did later in his career, to isolate the subject matter and treat it as if it were a still life. The prostitute is successful at her profession. Not only is she being offered money from a client, but two cheerful onlookers are also present. Yet there are a few pointers towards what is to come in his art in the carefully painted still life on the table and the elaborate carpet in disarray which makes a complicated pattern of colour. The carpet is seen again in the same state in the unloved and less popular picture in the Metropolitan Museum, New York, the *Interior with a Woman Asleep* (Plate 4). Modern museological propriety has prevented the picture's real title being used, for in the 1696 sale it was described as a drunken woman asleep at a table. The treatment of her face is surprisingly similar to that of the prostitute in *The Procuress*, but almost everything else is different. A single figure is now and for the first time seen in isolation, although not yet in a closed space. Instead, Vermeer lets us look for the only time into another room behind the partly open door. There

fig. 2 attributed to VERMEER
Esther before Ahasuerus
Canvas 173 × 261 cm.
Signed and dated upper left: Meer fecit 1654
Knokke-Zoute, Collection of Jean Decoen, lent to Tournai, Musée des Beaux-Arts

As far as is known this picture has not yet been subjected to laboratory analysis. Parts of it, especially the sky seen through the arch, are not in good condition, and nothing is at present known of the picture's earlier history.

fig. 3 attributed to VERMEER, after Felice Ficherelli
St. Praxedis
Canvas 103.5 × 84.5 cm.
Signed and dated lower left on the small stone leaning on the larger one: Meer· 1655
New York, with Spencer Samuels Inc.

The original painting by Ficherelli is in the Carlo del Bravo collection, Florence, and it is more than a little disconcerting that Vermeer should have copied such a picture. The saint's face is curiously reminiscent of the face of the sleeping woman in the Metropolitan Museum, New York (Plate 4).

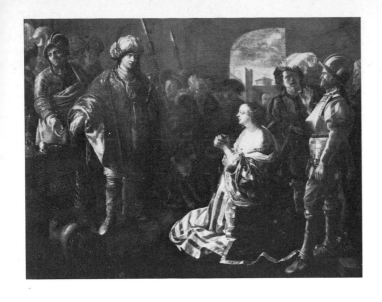

appears to be slight confusion on the table as the woman sleeps uncomfortably seated before her nearly empty glass.

From this stage of the artist's career there must be several pictures which are still missing. There are no works of transition which bring us towards the *Maidservant Pouring Milk* (Plate 7), and it must have required a period of constant experiment for the artist to reduce his scale so much and to change entirely his technique of painting.

One of the great enigmas of Vermeer's art, and there are several, is how he came to paint the two landscapes, one of which in terms of handling is clearly related to the *Maidservant Pouring Milk*. The texture of the brickwork in *The View of Delft* could almost be the bread on the table in the *Maidservant*. *The View of Delft* (Plate 5) has rightly moved and fascinated almost everybody who has seen it. It provoked some of Proust's most memorable passages, leading him to speculate on the inadequacy of his own achievement in comparison to even a small part of a picture such as *The View of Delft*. It is the endless reproductions which have reduced the picture to an irritatingly simple series of bands of sky, buildings, water and sand. They form a stratification beloved of the writers of manuals of how to paint pictures in three easy steps. What in fact happened, however, is that in this picture Vermeer took the whole art of landscape painting several stages further than it had yet gone and achieved a summit of perfection in this genre never equalled or surpassed. The conventions of his time were exacting. The art of townscape achieved a rigid order epitomised in the later seventeenth century in the work of Jan van der Heyden, while in Delft itself Pieter de Hoogh developed the painting of the courtyard scene to a point where he could go no further in the rendering of detail and atmosphere. Almost all Dutch townscape pictures, however, are in some way generalised; the atmosphere is distilled into the typical. This is precisely what Vermeer did not do. Instead he chose a specific moment. It is one of those days of cool air and alternating cloud and sunlight. The fretted Gothic spire of the Nieuwe Kerk is lit by a shaft of brilliant yellow sunlight while almost everything else, except a few rooftops, is in sombre shade. Each one of the thousand and more little individual details in the picture is observed exactly, and, yet, there is an atmospheric unity. The air is not quite still as the water trembles in the slight breeze which fragments the precise reflections of the complicated skyline.

The Little Street (Plate 6), in Amsterdam, is much less dazzling than *The View of Delft*. It is just a flat brick façade of a house in Delft seen on a dull day, and its very conventional quality invites the search for parallels amongst Vermeer's contemporaries in Delft. A few similar types of picture can be found, and one of them was painted by Jacobus Vrel, an artist whose career is

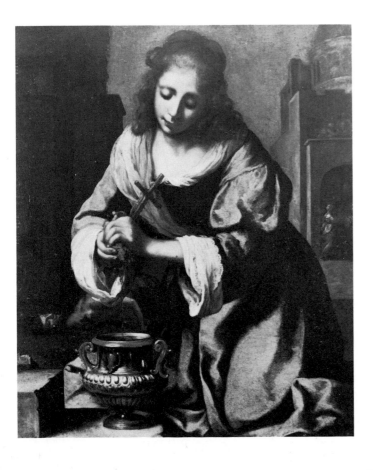

very much more in shadow than that of Vermeer himself. Vrel is believed to have worked in Delft in the 1660s and certainly painted several street scenes in addition to the interiors in which he specialised. In the example from the collection of the marquess of Bath at Longleat the same type of brick walls as in *The Little Street*, whitewashed to head height, are seen (fig. 4). Such a picture cannot be assumed to have been painted with a knowledge of Vermeer's art, but it does show a similar approach towards subject matter made at a similar time and place.

The *Maidservant Pouring Milk* (Plate 7), through the numerous reproductions, has been more popular with the public than any other picture of this type. Perhaps it is the unspoken moral endorsed by nineteenth century writers which has helped, for the picture is a perfect rendering of the dignity of work. Thus the nineteenth century could invoke the sentiment of 'He made them high and lowly and ordered their estate'. Small wonder that this picture has been taken as the epitome of domestic virtue, and reproductions of it have been in schoolrooms for generations. Of course the seventeenth century could not and did not think in these terms. Vermeer painted what he saw in front of him, a simple maidservant dressed in blue and yellow in the act of pouring milk. The picture does not glitter in the way that some of the later compositions resemble a stained glass window or medieval illuminated manuscript. Instead there is a solid intensity of contrasted blues and yellows not achieved in any other picture. If the assumptions so far made are correct, the *Maidservant Pouring Milk* is the first picture in which the artist exploited to the full the possibilities of light falling on a bare plaster wall. The little spots are not blotches on this or any other reproduction but minutely observed imperfections in the plaster.

The scale of Vermeer's pictures presents many problems in the reconstruction of his career. His early paintings up to and including *The Procuress* are on the large scale associated with Utrecht painting of the time, but *The View of Delft* shrinks in size while the *Maidservant Pouring Milk* is on the tiny scale he was to practise for most of the rest of his career. Occasionally, however, Vermeer remembered the grander scale of his early years and, for instance, produced the large scale *Artist's Studio* in his full maturity.

Quite closely related to the *Maidservant Pouring Milk* but much more sober in tone is the Dresden *Interior with a Girl at a Window Reading a Letter* (Plate 8). There is still considerable impasto, especially on the costume, but by comparison with *The Procuress*, in the same gallery, the surface has become smooth and enamel-like. In the same way as the *Maidservant Pouring Milk*, the *Girl Reading a Letter* is abstracted; she is not aware of the prying eyes of the artist. The cool, almost empty quality of the picture is relieved by the reflection of the

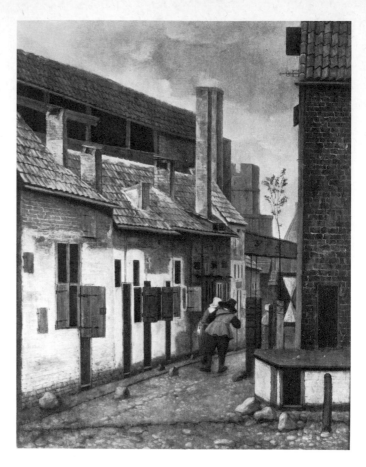

fig. 4 Jacobus VREL
Street Scene in [?] *Delft*
Canvas 35.5 × 26.5 cm.
Signed on the roof top at the left
Longleat House, Wiltshire, Collection of the marquess of Bath

Details of Vrel's life are still completely unknown. His pictures have a distinctive style, and some of them are signed.

girl's face in the partly open window in which we see almost full face her gentle expression distorted by the imperfections in the glass.

The shy character of the Dresden picture does not appear again until much later in the artist's career. Instead, he concentrated at this stage on interiors with two or more people in conversation. In the *Soldier with a Girl Laughing* (Plate 9) in the Frick Collection, New York, the girl is seen wearing exactly the same dress as the very different figure in the Dresden picture. Here she is laughing, while we are hardly permitted to see the face of the cavalier, who, presumably, has been the cause of her mirth. This is one of Vermeer's most strongly contrasted pictures as the dark silhouette of the cavalier is placed directly against the bright whiteness of the wall. A few touches of impasto remain, especially on the girl's dress, and for the first time Vermeer painted a map of the United Provinces. The present topography of the country is rather different as the Zuyder Zee was then very much larger, and it was the convention to orient the map with the coast running from east to west along the top instead of north to south.

After the almost brittle quality of the Frick picture the Berlin *Interior with a Gentleman and a Young Woman with a Wineglass* (Plate 10) appears much more sober. As might be expected the relationship between the figures has greater subtlety. The girl is draining her glass while the cavalier has his hand on the jug as if to offer to refill it. Already the artist had achieved a kind of quiet balance incipient in the Dresden *Girl Reading a Letter*, but he was to extend his preoccupation with balance and order in his pictures until the significance of the subject matter was so reduced that it almost disappeared entirely.

The *Girl Interrupted at her Music* (Plate 11), also in the Frick Collection, is one of the few pictures in which the girl seems to look straight out at the spectator while the man has Vermeer's more characteristic, abstracted quality. On the wall behind, just vaguely indicated, is a picture of Cupid which Vermeer must have owned as a dealer and collector, for it appears again, right at the end of his career, in the background of the London *Lady Standing at the Virginals* (Plate 33). Nobody can deny that the *Girl Interrupted at her Music* is damaged. It has lost much of its precision, but enough remains of the original surface to reveal many of Vermeer's special qualities. The cool light through the window falls on each object, transforming an ordinary room with two figures into a poetic harmony and disarming us because it appears so natural.

The same man, this time in a rather different mood, reappears in the Brunswick *Interior with Two Gentlemen and a Girl with a Wineglass* (Plate 12). Like the Frick painting this work has had a bad press. This is, perhaps, because it comes a little too near reality, and it lacks the sense of detachment favoured by the formal analysis school of critical writing. The mid-twentieth century reduced Vermeer's pictures to the geometry of the Cubism it had just discovered and was beginning to admire. The coquette in the Brunswick picture is too lively and her admirer a little too ardent in his attentions for this type of interpretation to hold water. To make matters worse, the whole of the background has been given, certainly no later than 1913, a coat of light mud colour in the name of restoration. The beautifully preserved figures and still life, therefore, jump uneasily from the now flat background. Of especial quality is the rose colour of the coquette's dress, contrasted with the cold bluish-white of the small cloth thrown casually over the deep blue tablecloth.

It is this contrast of colours which forms the leitmotif of the *Girl at a Window with a Jug* (Plate 13) in the Metropolitan Museum, New York. Here again Vermeer disarms us with apparent simplicity, but each and every object is arranged with precision in order to achieve an understated balance. The model seems naturally positioned between the window and the table, but it is quite obvious that the whole has been most carefully thought out. It is this unassuming character coupled with the perfection of the treatment of the light that make this one of Vermeer's best pictures. The artist, however, did not take this particular aspect of his interests any further but, instead, went on to experiment in a very different way.

The Windsor *Music Lesson* and the Boston *Concert*, while certainly not a pair of pictures, come together as two highly complex works which are very similar to one another. They both seem to develop quite naturally out of the Brunswick *Interior* but with the major difference of the decline in the importance of the subject matter.

The Music Lesson (Plate 14) has a very special place in Vermeer's art. It seems to be in almost perfect condition. The blues have perished a little and have become slightly more grey in tone, but there is definitely no feeling of looking through a veil of incompetent retouching which many an arrogant restorer has put on some of Vermeer's pictures in the name of improvement. *The Music Lesson* has, in fact, no obvious subject. Nineteenth century criticism wanted to turn it into a music lesson but no such event is taking place. The girl is looking down at the virginals—we cannot see whether she is actually playing—while the man stands by her side with an indifferent expression on his face. So we are left with the very twentieth century view that the picture's subject does not matter. The Boston *Concert* (Plate 15) has much less of this quality, and it is also less precise. In both pictures there is a feeling of sumptuousness and opulence, almost an optical illusion as, in fact, both rooms are cold and bare. In *The Music Lesson* the tiles on the floor have a bluish cast while the marks which the plasterer left on the wall at the back have been exactly recorded by the artist. Indeed if we could go back into one of Vermeer's rooms we would find it cold and uncomfortable. The only warmth in contrast to the bare plaster and cold tile would have been the odd chair and the carpets, draped over tables as they were considered far too precious to put on the floor.

Vermeer's mature career went through several obvious changes but nobody so far has produced a convincing account of how this happened. There is a whole group of pictures which are much softer in character than *The Music Lesson*, and perhaps the almost soft-edged figure on the right of *The Concert* is a herald of this, although it has to be admitted that there is no real precedent for the near melting quality of the Frick *Lady with her Maid* (Plate 17).

Possibly the first picture in this group is the Washington *Interior with a Lady Writing a Letter* (Plate 16). She is seen wearing the ample yellow coat trimmed with ermine which appears in so many of Vermeer's pictures right until the end of his career. Her attitude is reminiscent of, but not identical to, the young woman on the right of the Boston *Concert*. Similar too is the slightly blurred way in which the pictures on the wall are handled in both pictures. As the *Lady Writing a Letter* was isolated for long in a collection in the Bahamas, it escaped the serious attention of many European critics. In a quiet way it sums up this aspect of Vermeer's art, the fragile moment when the woman looks up quizzically, as if she has been disturbed from the private pleasure of writing a letter.

The same yellow coat appears very much more dramatically in the Frick *Lady with her Maid* (Plate 17). This unique picture has been under something of a critical cloud, without its authenticity being rejected, although Gowing's second thoughts (*Johannes Vermeer*, 1961, p. 25) were obviously intended to be taken seriously, as he removed the picture from Vermeer's oeuvre altogether. The background is lost in an uncharacteristic gloom while the large scale of the figures is reminiscent of the artist's early work. These two differences apart, Vermeer has managed with the simplest of means to create a world new to him. The maid is a very solid creature, so often found in the work of Nicolas Maes, while her mistress is unusually gaudy. Her hair is extravagantly adorned, her pearl earring is over-large, and her yellow coat somehow assumes a dominance in the picture. But it is the contrast between this dominant yellow and the pale blue of the tablecloth seen against the violent ultramarine of the maid's skirt which makes this picture extreme in Vermeer's art, for here he took a big step from his closed world and produced, this once, a glitter which is uncharacteristic.

The four surviving heads, all of women, painted by Vermeer have suffered both over-admiration and critical neglect. They are not as closely related as

reproductions might suggest, but the soft texture of the Frick *Lady with her Maid* certainly is to be found in the Hague *Girl with a Pearl Earring* (Plate 19). This famous picture has often been compared with the *Portrait of a Young Woman* (Plate 18) which is now in a private collection in New York. In terms of the handling of the paint the two pictures differ. Neither is in perfect condition, although the Hague picture, perhaps, has been over-praised, while the privately owned one has been thought to be in a worse state than, in fact, it is. The latter is less glamorous than its more famous counterpart, and, yet, so much of what is admired in Vermeer is there. She exists in a world of her own, with a self-contained quality which gives Thoré-Bürger's extravagant comparison with the *Mona Lisa* some justification. Her gentle smile is an eternal enigma; she is the sphinx without a secret.

The *Girl with a Pearl Earring* is much more direct, less mysterious, but the picture has suffered much. There is that same impenetrable background exactly as in the Frick *Lady with her Maid*, and so we must be content with a shadow of what must have been in the partly open lips and almost come-hither gaze.

Very different in style are the two *Heads* (Plates 20 and 21) in Washington. Often considered a pair, they are Vermeer's only surviving paintings on panel. Both pictures contain characteristics unusual for Vermeer, and this has led some modern scholars to doubt them as authentic, little masterpieces though the pictures are. As the history of *The Girl in a Red Hat* can be traced at least to 1822, it must have been painted before this first recorded appearance, and, on grounds of style and quality, these *Heads* find a place among Vermeer's best work. It is almost as if the artist abandoned his enigmatic closed quality in order to make the two figures appeal directly to the spectator. The dots of light paint describing form have progressed to the extreme, especially in *The Girl in a Red Hat*, while the tapestry background in both pictures is similar in handling to the scenes on the map in the background of *The Artist's Studio*.

As with the two *Heads*, doubts have also been cast upon the *Interior with a Woman Playing the Lute* (Plate 22) in the Metropolitan Museum, New York. This could be caused by the picture's condition. The composition, however, is unmistakably that of Vermeer, although we are looking at a melancholy shadow. Vermeer's spirit, nevertheless, shines through, and enough is left of the harmony of blue and yellow, made all the more intense by the grey-white of the wall, to make this a very touching picture. The woman's gaze is particularly serene.

The *Lady Reading a Letter* (Plate 23) at Amsterdam is near perfectly preserved and can give some idea of what has been lost in the New York picture. Just part of the map is visible on the wall this time. Only those who

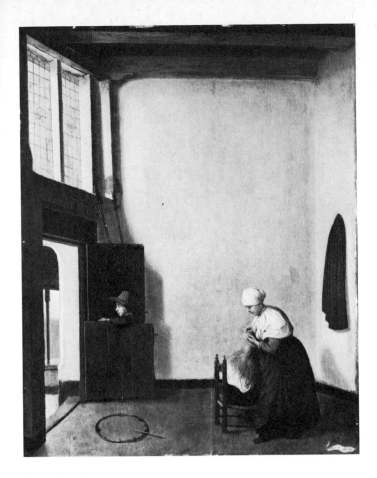

fig. 5 Jacobus VREL
Interior with a Woman Combing a Child's Hair
Panel 53 × 41 cm.
Detroit, Institute of Arts

In a picture of this type Vrel achieved a sense
of detachment rare in seventeenth century
Dutch painting. He surely knew Vermeer;
it would have been difficult for the artists to
avoid each other in Delft.

have seen this picture in the original can realise one
point which is an occasional, but near miraculous
characteristic of Vermeer. This is the afterglow which is
introduced where the colour is especially intense.
The woman's coat is, in fact, quite a light blue which,
in shadow, acquires a peculiar intensity radiating
beyond the woman's back silhouetted against the wall.
Here, Vermeer introduced a pale afterglow which
increases the illusion of three dimensions. The picture
is basically a harmony in blue and various shades of
ochre, and it is very cold in tone.

Quite closely related but remarkable for the absence
of blue is the Berlin *Interior with a Young Woman with a
Pearl Necklace* (Plate 24). It is in this picture that the
blank wall plays its largest role, and Vermeer dared to
place absolutely nothing on it. Again, the work of the
mysterious Jacobus Vrel springs to mind, for in his
Interior with a Woman Combing a Child's Hair (fig. 5)
in the Detroit Institute of Arts, Vrel, like Vermeer,
took the risk of devoting almost half the picture to a
blank wall. Vrel, of course, never had his fellow citizen's
mastery of light, so we can only admire his composition
and speculate as to how both artists arrived at this
exquisite extreme at the same time. The Berlin picture
reproduces badly, giving a feeling of emptiness when,
in fact, quite the opposite is true. The build up of still
life at the left is particularly opulent with the oriental
style vase and the elaborately wrought chair-back.
It is the woman's face and neck, however, which demand
attention, as she seems to be delighting in the cold light
pouring in from the window and falling on her precious
pearls.

The Washington *Interior with a Woman Weighing Gold*
(Plate 25) heralds a new departure in Vermeer's art, a
departure which was to end, sadly, in the very obvious
Allegory of Faith (Plate 34). In this picture, however, the
element of allegory is much more subtle, for it is perfectly
natural that a well-dressed lady should be weighing
gold—or are they pearls?—in an interior. It is, however,
not perfectly natural that she should be silhouetted
against a dramatic picture, reminiscent in style of
Abraham Bloemaert or Joachim Wttewael, of *The
Last Judgement*. The weighing of souls as a separate
subject is found frequently in Medieval and Renais-
sance art, but Vermeer produced his allegory by
depicting a very ordinary scene and making the entire
point by the device of the picture on the wall.

The increasing shadows of the Washington picture
anticipate in style Vermeer's only surviving pair of
pendants, *The Astronomer* (Plate 26) and *The Geographer*
(Plate 27). *The Astronomer*, perfect, is still privately
owned, while *The Geographer* exists in an overpainted
and damaged state at Frankfurt. Both pictures appear
to use the same model in the same room with similar
furniture and accessories. *The Astronomer* is dated
1668 while *The Geographer*, genuinely signed, also

bears a reconstructed or falsely added signature and the date '1669'. Whoever put the date on this picture, and it was not Vermeer, could have been recording, more or less accurately, what was there before.

The Astronomer is one of Vermeer's most mysterious and atmospheric pictures but *The Geographer* is much more lively. The room is bathed in daylight, and he looks up from his work as if disturbed. Rembrandt's etching of *Faust* often has been compared to this picture as a source for Vermeer's composition, but the etching has to be reversed for the comparison to be valid. Perhaps there was a Rembrandt painting of the subject, now lost, which Vermeer knew.

The Astronomer provides, for the first time since *The Procuress*, a welcome starting point, in this case for the reconstruction of Vermeer's last phase. His final paintings, which have to be regarded as a decline, are relatively easy to distinguish but the neglected *Astronomer* and *Geographer*, because they lack the ease and perfection of such pictures as the Amsterdam *Lady Reading a Letter*, have been taken as a herald of that decline. This is unfair because what in fact seems to have happened is that the artist continued to experiment with ever clearer colours, combined with intense shadows, a path which eventually led to the Amsterdam *Lady Reading a Letter with her Maid* (Plate 29).

One of the fundamental questions which has never been solved about this stage in Vermeer's art is the date of what must be seen as the central act of his career, *The Artist's Studio* (Plate 28) in Vienna. That it is a mature work nobody has ever doubted, and many of the conventions it introduces, for example the artistically draped curtain at the left, appear only in the last pictures.

It is impossible to say when in the 1660s Vermeer produced this masterpiece. Although *The Astronomer* and *The Geographer* provide a relatively firm anchor for his style in the late 1660s, they are not sufficiently similar to *The Artist's Studio* to date that picture definitely c. 1668/69. There are certain points of resemblance, however, especially in the handling of the still life on the table which appears in all three pictures.

The Artist's Studio exists on many different levels, firstly as an outright triumph of pure painting. So many times Vermeer causes us to marvel at his near miraculous technique, but here it is as if he included in one picture everything he had learned in his career. The chandelier, for instance, foreshadows in its pointillist intensity all the magical picture frames which appear in his late work, while the map on the wall sums up all the other maps which he so lovingly had painted. The model herself, in the way the light falls from the unseen window, has a purity rarely achieved in his other pictures. Then there is the painter himself. Tantalisingly he is seen from behind, and we shall never know whether it is Vermeer himself or a model posing as an artist. This simple picture of an artist's studio has also been interpreted as an allegory of painting. This is not unreasonable as the artist is seen painting a figure dressed in an allegorical attitude.

After *The Artist's Studio*, the still wonderful *Interior with a Lady with her Maid* (Plate 29) at Amsterdam appears almost as an anticlimax. Yet the picture is too easily dismissed as it represents an exciting experiment in the handling of the extreme effects of light. Almost two-thirds of the picture is lost in deep shadows which serve to contrast with and intensify the brilliantly lit interior. There is a certain harshness, and the tiles on the floor no longer seem solid but appear to be what they really are, areas of flat paint. The figures are on a tiny scale, forming a maze of intricate patterns of brilliantly coloured light, while the familiar yellow coat is more strident than ever.

The Beit *Interior with a Lady Writing a Letter with her Maid* (Plate 30) is broken up in an even more geometrical manner than the Amsterdam picture, but its sense of order and sober tonality recall the Washington *Woman Weighing Gold* (Plate 25). The picture has lost some of the subtlety we have come to expect, while the gaze of the standing maid has some of that oversimplified character which disconcerts us in the Kenwood *Guitar Player* (Plate 32). It is unfair to be too severe with the Beit picture as it also has many of Vermeer's best qualities. The figure of the lady writing is quite up to the standard of and close in style to the celebrated *Lacemaker* (Plate 31) in the Louvre. It is almost surprising that such a small picture in such a large picture gallery can make so great an impact on the unsuspecting visitor. Because the scale is so small each part can be studied with ease. The woman's expression is at the same time both concentrated and relaxed while she executes her complicated task of lacemaking. She wears her hair in a series of exaggerated curls which appear again in extreme form in the Kenwood *Guitar Player* (Plate 32), and it seems reasonable to assume that *The Lacemaker* is also a late picture.

The light in *The Lacemaker* envelops the whole without having any particular source. The artist's supreme control in the handling of light and texture is nowhere better seen than in the London *Lady Standing at the Virginals* (Plate 33). It is an uneasy picture in spite of being one of the artist's greatest achievements detail by detail. The painting of the woman's dress has long been recognized as a tour de force of observation. Vermeer made it appear as if she is actually playing the virginals as her hands are blurred as they slip over the keys. The unexpected painting of a prematurely obese Cupid is somewhat uncomfortably juxtaposed against her head, but the background wall has on it another of Vermeer's triumphs in the rendering of the gilded picture frame.

It is a similar gilded frame which illuminates the

Kenwood *Guitar Player* (Plate 32). Again, it has to be admitted that this is not one of Vermeer's best pictures. There is almost a sense of weariness as if he had played out his passion for light on walls and costumes. The woman's dress is hard and metallic instead of being crisp and perfect as in the *Lady Standing at the Virginals*. The picture is saved by the gilded frame. The landscape inside the frame has puzzled many people, and it has been attributed rather optimistically to Jan Wynants, who never painted in so bold a manner. If Vermeer had chosen to paint a wooded landscape, as indeed Jan van der Heyden was to do when he grew tired of town-scape, it would surely have looked rather like the painting on the wall, cold and empty but perfectly balanced.

It is a commonly held notion that artists improve in their last years. Those painters like Titian and Rembrandt who lived into old age were able to sum up their careers and create a new, free style with a very strong emotional content. This cannot be true for artists of Vermeer's type for whom everything relies on precise control. We do not know if Vermeer's health declined seriously when he was in his late thirties, but certainly there was an ever-growing family coupled with increasing poverty. Logically this would have led him to increase his output, but his last pictures have every evidence of his usual painstaking care. They were painted very precisely but seem to have lost the sense of order which is such an essential part of his mature pictures.

An Allegory of Faith (Plate 34) in the Metropolitan Museum, New York, has in its individual parts much of Vermeer's usual quality, yet the overall effect is unpleasant. Perhaps we really cannot accept the obvious Roman Catholic allegory which probably reflects Vermeer's own religious beliefs. The Sacraments are painted with just the same detachment as in the earlier pictures, but with the difference that every object in this cluttered room is there for a specific iconographic reason. What looks like Eve's fruit lies partly eaten on the floor, and near to it writhes the serpent, crushed, with a stream of blood issuing from its mouth.

There will always be disagreement as to which picture is actually the last we have from Vermeer's hand. The London *Lady Seated at the Virginals* (Plate 35) must be very near the end. The picture suffers from being hung close to the *Lady Standing at the Virginals* (Plate 33), and the comparison is unfortunate. The seated woman's dress is particularly summary in treatment, but it would be unfair to dismiss this work as altogether inferior. In the background hangs Baburen's *Procuress* (fig. 11, see p. 80). The original picture, which Vermeer must have owned, as it appears, less clearly, in the background of the Boston *Concert* (Plate 15), is now in the Museum of Fine Arts at Boston. Baburen's

Procuress was also the subject of a dangerous forgery by van Meegeren (fig. 12), now hanging in the Courtauld Institute, London, as a warning to the unwary. It is, perhaps, a little strange that Vermeer should have depicted his Baburen so lovingly at a time when it would have been quite out of fashion. Vermeer also introduced into this picture the blurred hands familiar from the *Lady Standing at the Virginals*.

From the point of view of the critic's desire to have everything neatly slotted into place it would be much more satisfactory if the *Lady Seated at the Virginals* clearly concluded Vermeer's career. There is, however, one more surprise in store, the little *Lady at the Virginals* (Plate 36), formerly in the Beit collection. Few scholars have been able to make up their minds about this minuscule object but even from reproduction it is so near to Vermeer's spirit that it surely must be his last surviving effort. Again the hands are blurred. The woman wears yellow, and there is also the characteristic metallic quality of her dress and the familiar exaggerated curls. If we try to judge this picture against the standards of Vermeer's best work we come away disillusioned, but if we see it as a last attempt, before death overtook him at the age of forty-three, the picture has a touching and intimate feeling which the scepticism of critics cannot erase.

Any attempt to place Vermeer in the context of his own time must begin by emphasizing his uniqueness. His idiosyncratic way of painting is a likely reason for his failure in the eyes of his contemporaries. It is possible that he used optical aids to construct his pictures, and these probably took the form of a kind of light box, but of all this we cannot be sure as there is no evidence. Such pictures as the *Allegory of Faith* show that Vermeer occasionally was able to conform to the taste of his time in terms of his subject matter but never in his way of seeing. Vermeer could never have painted in the manner of the brilliantly successful Gerard Dou however much he may have wanted to for financial reasons.

In the early 1670s the United Provinces went through a difficult period, and the war with Louis XIV with its accompanying financial problems meant that there was less money to be spent on the luxury of pictures. Secondly, there was a very definite change in fashion, and, paradoxically, collectors wanted pictures painted in the more elaborate French manner. Landscapes acquired classical overtones, and genre scenes drew increasingly upon religious, moral or allegorical subject matter. Vermeer died just at the moment when these changes were beginning to be felt, and the *Allegory of Faith*, perhaps, can be seen as an attempt to keep up with the new trends.

The main problem which confuses every attempt to reconstruct the sequence of artistic endeavour in the Delft of Vermeer's time is the absence of dates on the pictures and the existence of only scanty documentation. Carel Fabritius dated his *View of Delft* in the National Gallery, London, 1654, the year he was killed, but it bears no resemblance whatever to Vermeer's treatment of the same subject (Plate 5). From the point of view of Vermeer's stylistic affinity with Pieter de Hoogh, we are on slightly safer ground. De Hoogh worked in Delft from 1654 until approximately 1663, by which time he was in Amsterdam, and it was in Delft that he produced his best pictures. They were much admired in the nineteenth century but today he has declined in public estimation. His pictures are perfectly balanced, finely detailed and atmospheric, but show no real interest in the fall of light in the manner which preoccupied Vermeer. The similarities and the differences between the two artists are emphasized by de Hoogh's *Woman Weighing Gold* (fig. 6) in Berlin. From the point of view of subject matter, composition and even colour, de Hoogh comes tantalizingly close to Vermeer, but the picture hangs in close proximity to the *Woman with a Pearl Necklace* (Plate 24), bathed in a clear cool light, while, in comparison, the de Hoogh seems to have a solid, almost clay-like quality in spite of the beauty of its colour and texture.

Vermeer has provokéd many responses from many different critics, some of them brilliant writers. Scholarship, on the other hand, has failed to produce very much of significance, and most of what is useful is due to Thoré-Bürger. It is, therefore, hardly surprising that much of what has been written about Vermeer is literary in content. Words, however, seem inadequate in front of the pictures themselves.

What Vermeer distilled in those thirty-five or so pictures, most of which are quite small, even tiny, gives him a special place not so much in his own time, when he was ignored, but outside it. Vermeer has taken his place in the history of the taste of the last hundred years, and from the strictly historical point of view he hardly should be mentioned since he was of so little importance in the intensely active time in which he lived. A modern parallel is that there may be a housewife in Luton or Llandudno whose pictures, unknown in their time outside the walls of the local art society, will assume a significant place in the artistic scene of the twenty-third century to come. Vermeer has become part of twentieth century culture. The present has edited the past to its liking and relegated to second and third place such establishment artists of the seventeenth century as Cornelis van Haarlem and Bloemaert. Vermeer is now seen as the purest expression of the Dutch spirit. The very fact that he is unique is part of the attraction. Thus, we can for ever ask ourselves, standing in front of *The View of Delft* or *The Artist's Studio* how is it that one ordinary human being could have said so much in so small a space by arranging little areas of colour on a piece of canvas?

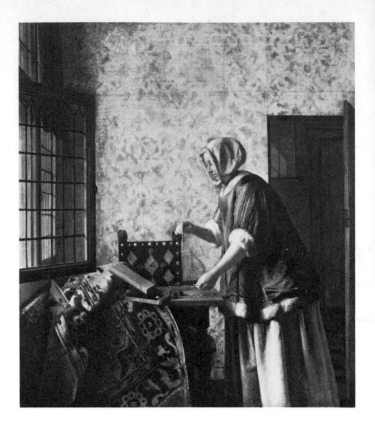

fig. 6 Pieter de HOOGH
Interior with a Woman Weighing Gold
Canvas 61 × 53 cm.
Berlin-Dahlem, Staatliche Gemäldegalerie

This is a perfect picture in every way except that the artist did not have Vermeer's mastery over light. Unfortunately Pieter de Hoogh has been neglected in recent years as the anecdotal character of much of his art has not met with the approval of mid-twentieth century art criticism.

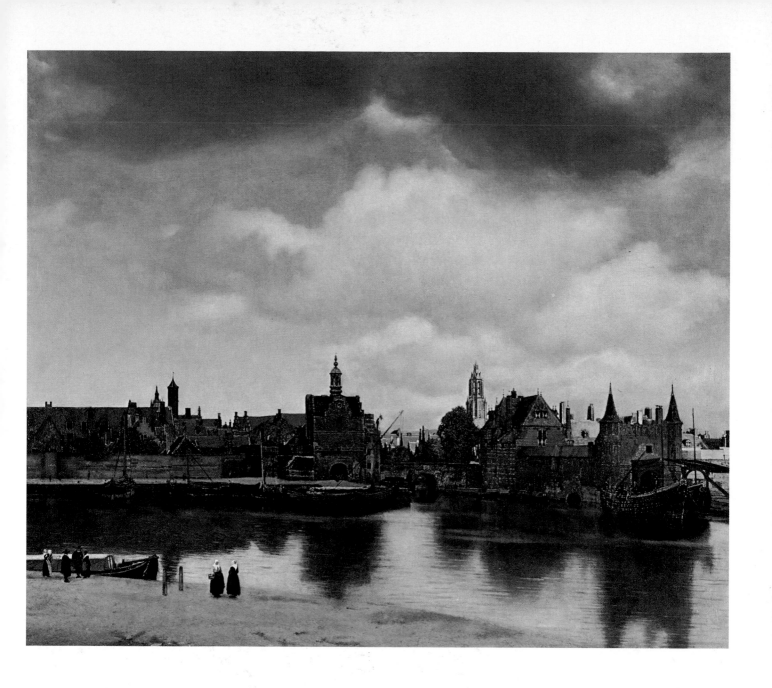

I *The View of Delft* (Plate 5)
The Hague, Mauritshuis

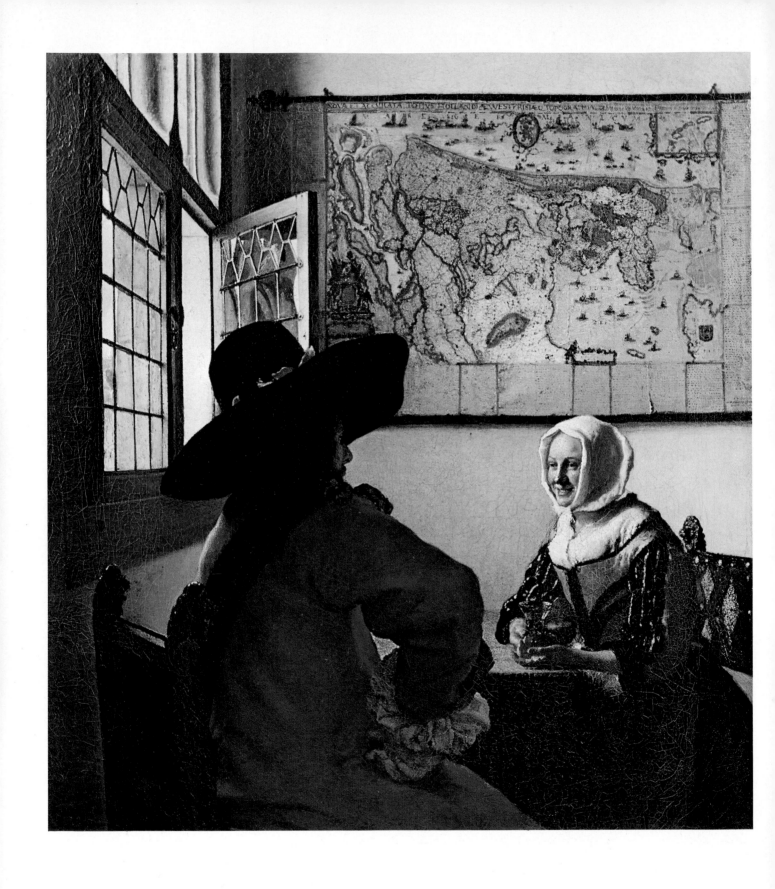

II *Interior with a Soldier and a Girl Laughing* (Plate 9)
New York, Frick Collection

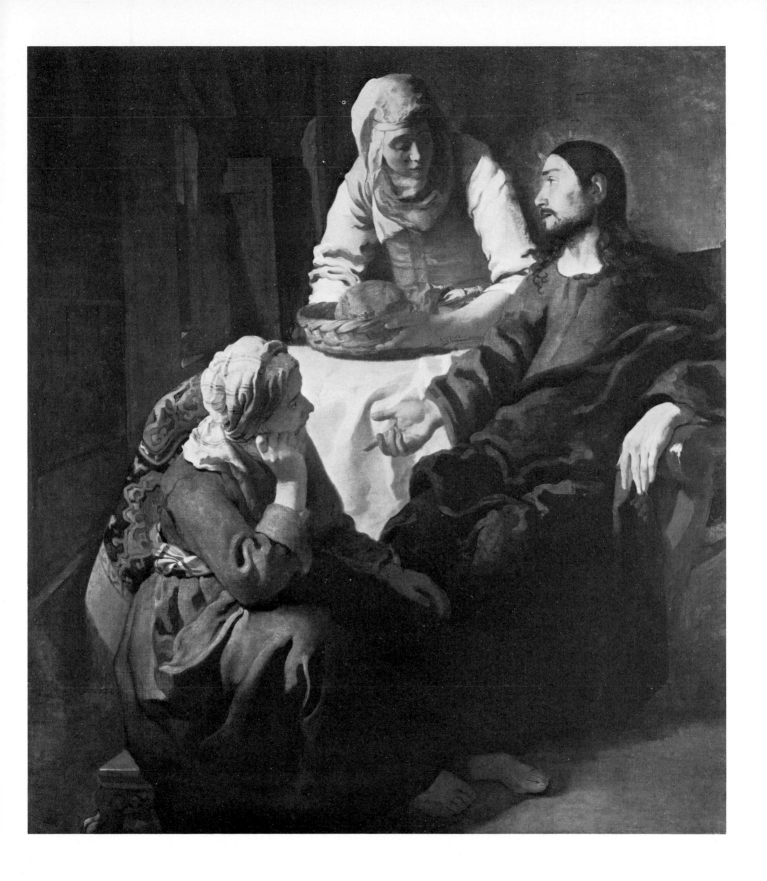

1 *Christ in the House of Martha and Mary*
EDINBURGH, National Gallery of Scotland. Canvas 160 × 142 cm. Signed on the edge of the stool at the left: IVMEER

Even the nineteenth century history of this picture is obscure. The painting could well have formed part of the celebrated Miles collection at Leigh Court, near Bristol, although it does not appear in the catalogue of that collection drawn up in 1822. It was certainly on the Bristol art market just before 1900, and then changed hands in London. By 1901 it was in the Coats collection at Skelmorlie Castle, Scotland, where it remained until it was given to the National Gallery of Scotland in 1927 by Mr. Coats's two sons in memory of their father.

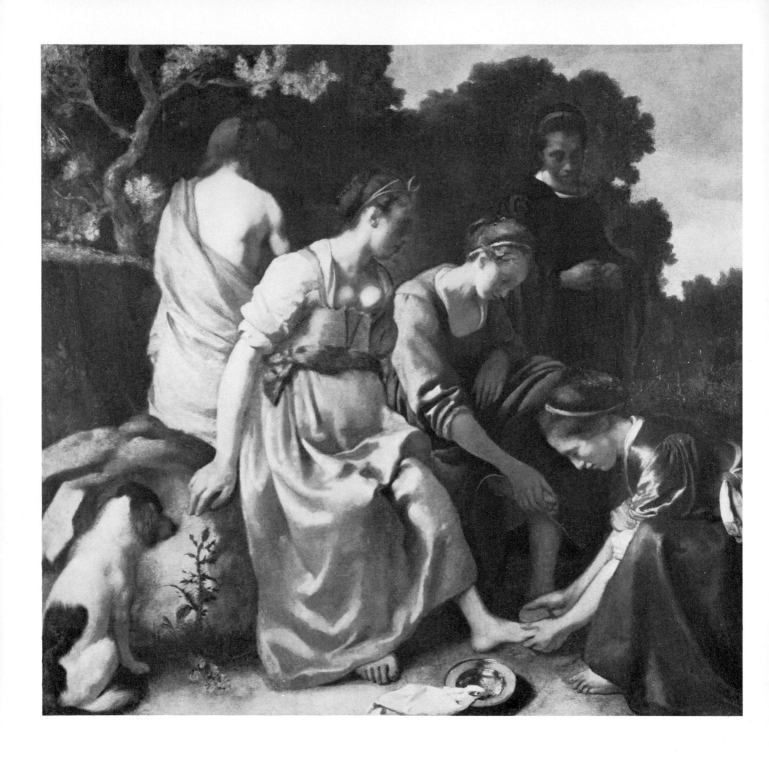

2 *Diana and her Companions*
THE HAGUE, Mauritshuis. Canvas 98.5 × 105 cm. The signature was formerly visible on the rock at the left: JvMeer

Diana and her Companions went unrecorded until the middle of the nineteenth century when it was in the collection of Neville D. Goldsmid at The Hague. It was sold in Paris in 1876 as by Nicolas Maes and was acquired by the Mauritshuis in the same year. Hofstede de Groot was virtually certain of the picture's authenticity as by Vermeer, remarking on its poor condition and the clumsy attempts to alter the signature into that of Maes and comparing it to the *Christ in the House of Martha and Mary* (Plate 1). The picture is in almost ruined condition. Many of the details, especially the faces, are very blurred through rubbing.

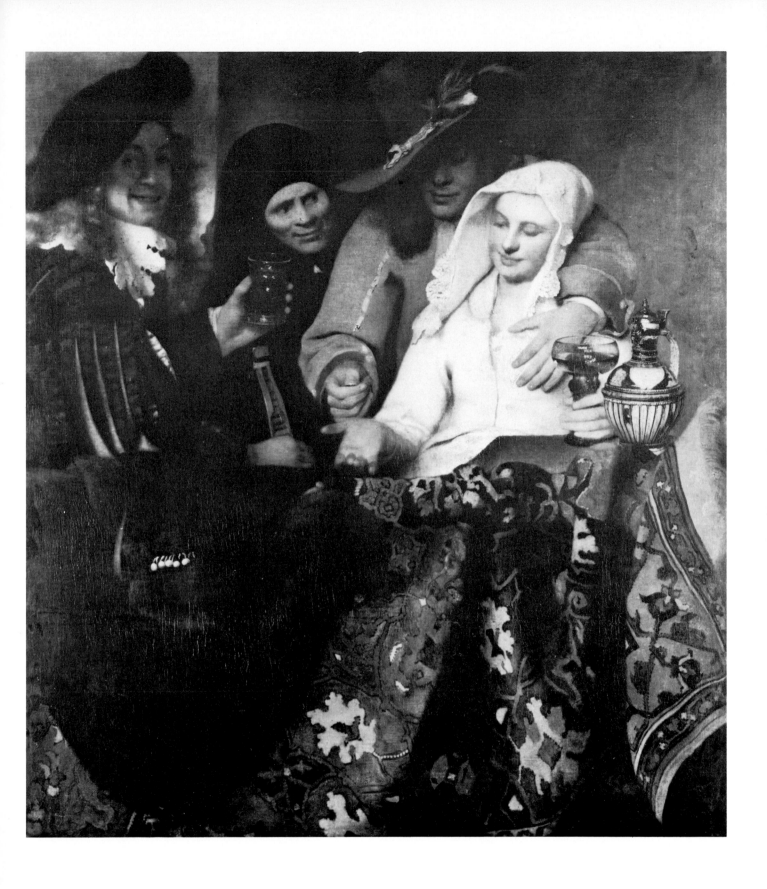

3   *The Procuress*
DRESDEN, Staatliche Gemäldegalerie. Canvas 143 × 130 cm. Signed and dated lower right: J. V.
MEER 1656

Quite possibly this picture was lot 9 in the 1696 sale, but the first certain record dates from its
acquisition in 1741, by Augustus III, Elector of Saxony and King of Poland, from the Wallenstein
collection at Dux. The picture has been in the Dresden gallery ever since except for a brief period
after 1945. It was ascribed to 'J. Vermeer' as early as 1835, and it was definitely attributed to
Vermeer of Delft by both Waagen and Thoré-Bürger in 1859.

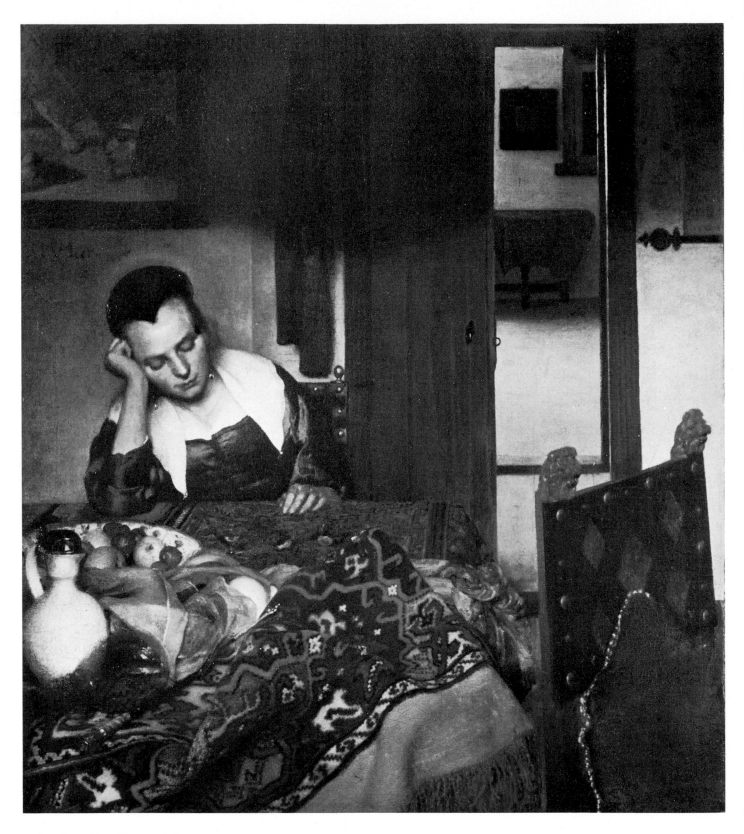

4 *Interior with a Woman Asleep*
NEW YORK, Metropolitan Museum of Art (Bequest of Benjamin Altman). Canvas 85 × 73.5 cm.
Signed on the upper left wall below the picture: I V Meer

In the 1696 sale the picture was described as 'Een dronke slapende Meyde aen een Tafel', and from
the almost empty wineglass it can be assumed that the woman, indeed, is sleeping off the effects of
too much alcohol. The subsequent history of this picture is uncertain. It was sold in Amsterdam
in 1735 when it was described simply as a sleeping woman and did not appear again until 1881
when it was in the Paris sale of John W. Wilson. By 1898 it was in the hands of the important
Paris dealer Sedelmeyer, but by 1907 the picture had been acquired by Duveen from Rodolph
Kann, Paris. Duveen sold the picture immediately to Benjamin Altman, who, in turn, bequeathed
it to the Metropolitan Museum in 1913.

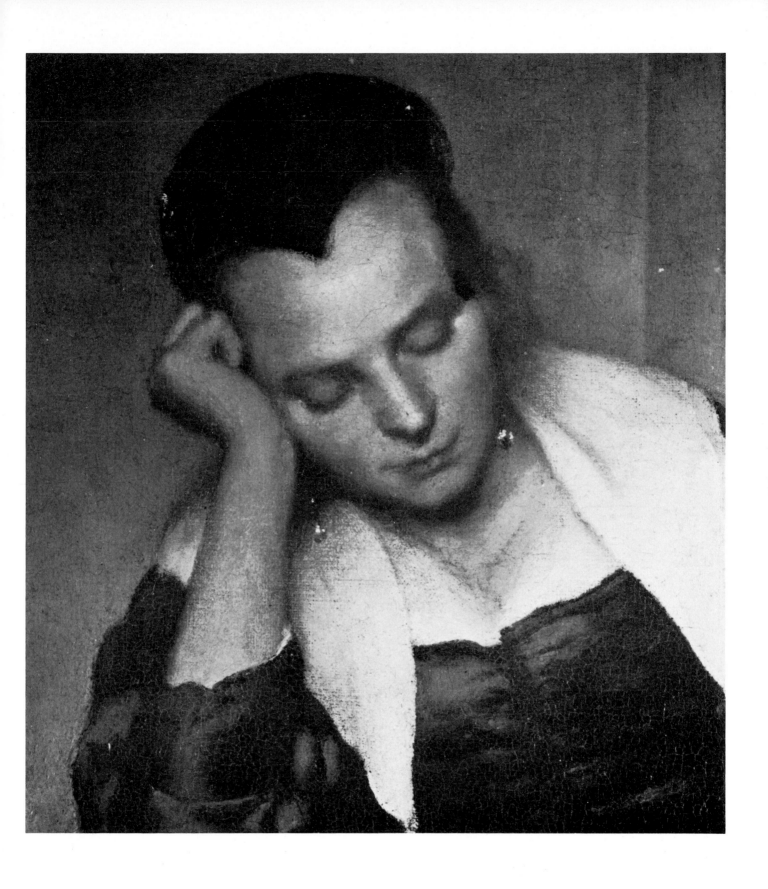

Interior with a Woman Asleep (detail)

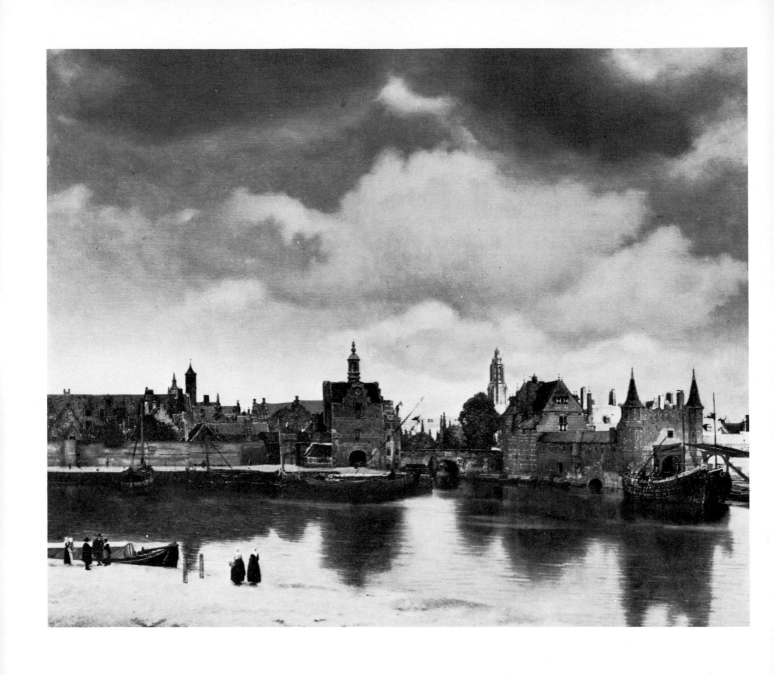

5 *The View of Delft*
THE HAGUE, Mauritshuis. Canvas 98.5 × 117.5 cm. Signed in monogram on the boat: JvM

Sold for the highest price, 200 florins, at the 1696 sale, *The View of Delft* subsequently was lost sight of until its sale in Amsterdam in 1822, when it was acquired by the Dutch Government for the considerable sum of 2900 florins. Even at this date, when Vermeer's reputation simply did not exist, *The View of Delft* was considered enough of a masterpiece to warrant state intervention. It was then placed in the Royal Picture Gallery (The Mauritshuis), where it has been the object of admiration and veneration ever since.

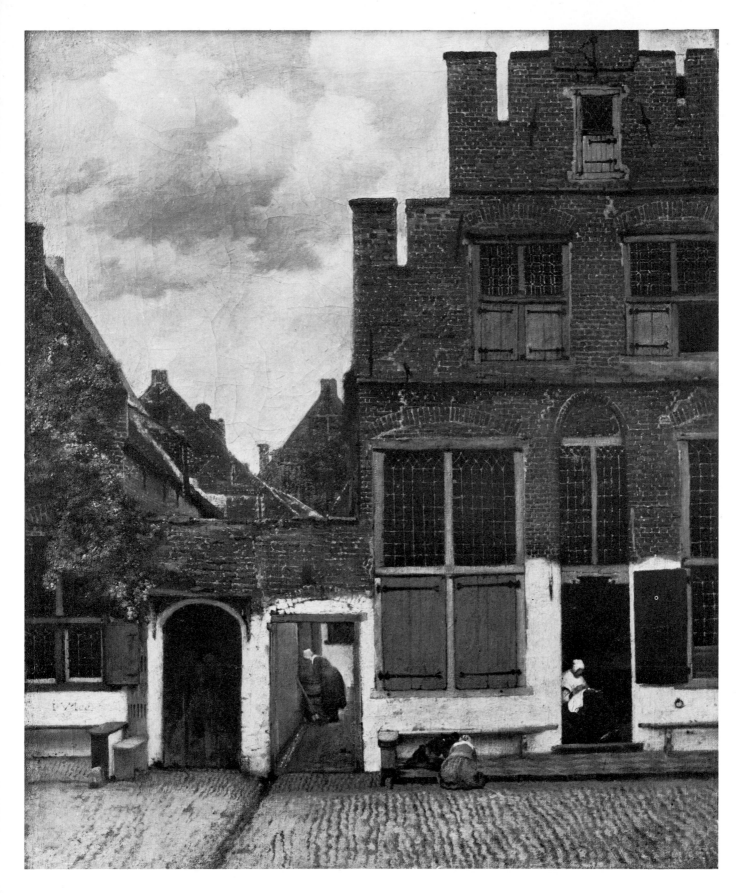

6 *A Street in Delft (The Little Street)*

AMSTERDAM, Rijksmuseum. Canvas 53.4 × 44 cm. Signed on the whitewashed wall underneath the window at the left: JvMeer

Almost certainly in the 1696 sale as lot 32 or possibly lot 33, the picture was described there as a view of a house in Delft. It did not appear again until an Amsterdam sale in 1800 and was then in the van Winter collection, Amsterdam, and later in the famous Six collection there. *The Little Street* was given to the Rijksmuseum by Sir Henry Deterding in 1921.

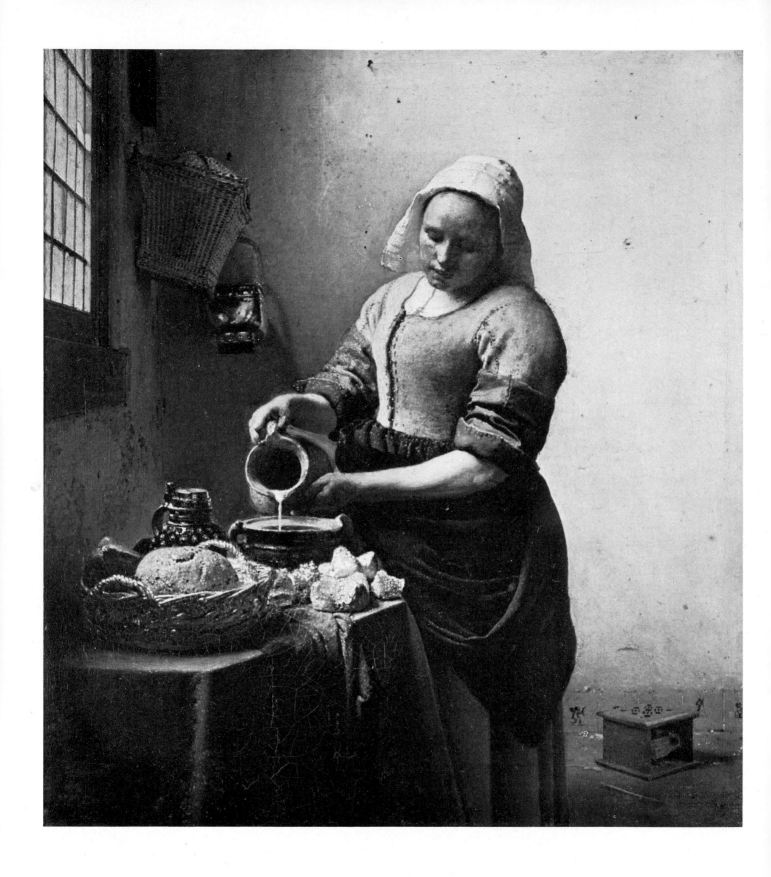

7 *Interior with a Maidservant Pouring Milk* (*The Milkmaid*)
AMSTERDAM, Rijksmuseum. Canvas 45.5 × 41 cm. Described by Hofstede de Groot as signed 'J v
Meer', but this is not visible today.

In the 1696 sale as lot 2, the picture made the relatively high price of 175 florins, only a little less
than *The View of Delft*. It appeared frequently in sales in Amsterdam in the eighteenth century,
in 1701, 1719, 1765 and 1768. The picture was seen by Sir Joshua Reynolds on his visit to The
Netherlands in 1781, when it bore an attribution to 'D. Vandermeere', and was sold again in
Amsterdam in 1798 and 1813. It was then in the Six collection along with *The Little Street* (Plate 6)
and was acquired by the Rijksmuseum in 1907/08.

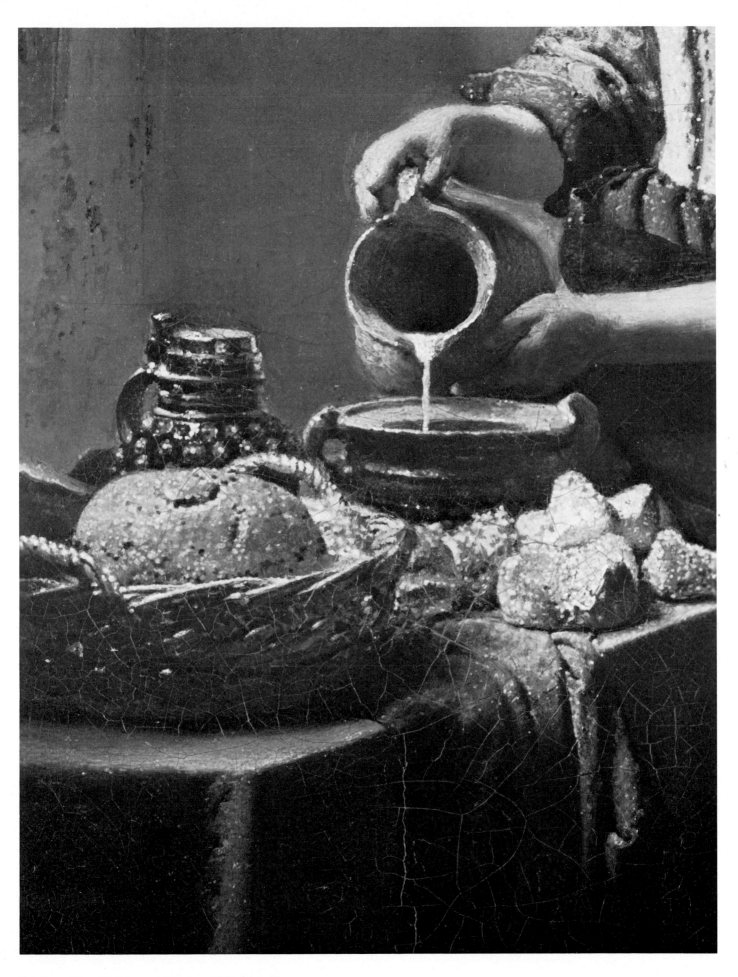

Interior with a Maidservant Pouring Milk (detail)

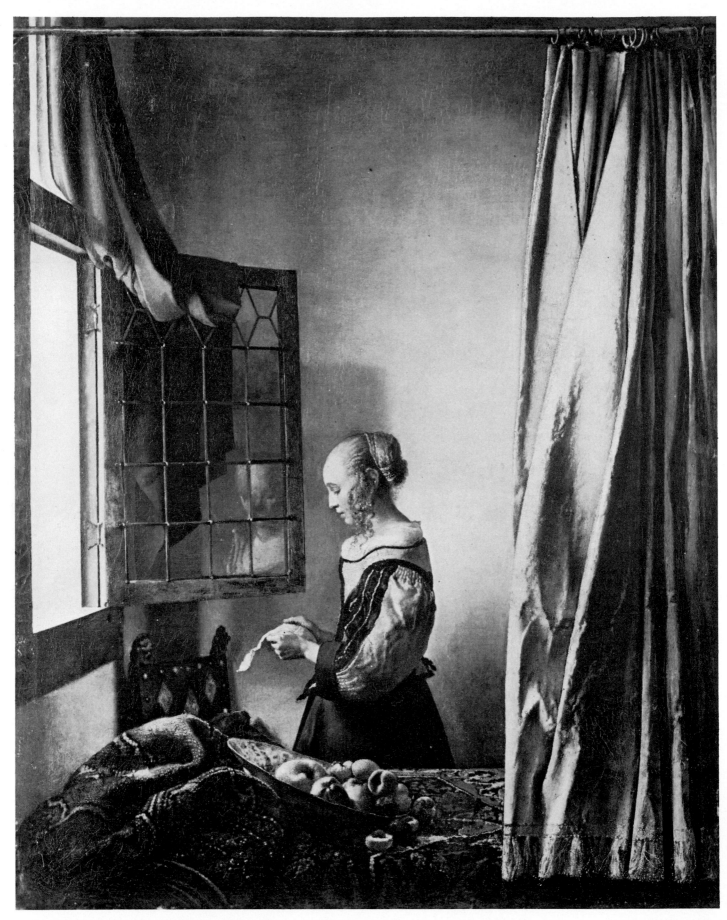

8 *Interior with a Girl at a Window Reading a Letter*
DRESDEN, Staatliche Gemäldegalerie. Canvas 83 × 64.5 cm. In 1862 Thoré-Bürger recorded that traces of a signature which read 'Meer' were visible in the background.

The picture was acquired by Augustus III of Saxony-Poland for his Dresden picture gallery in 1742

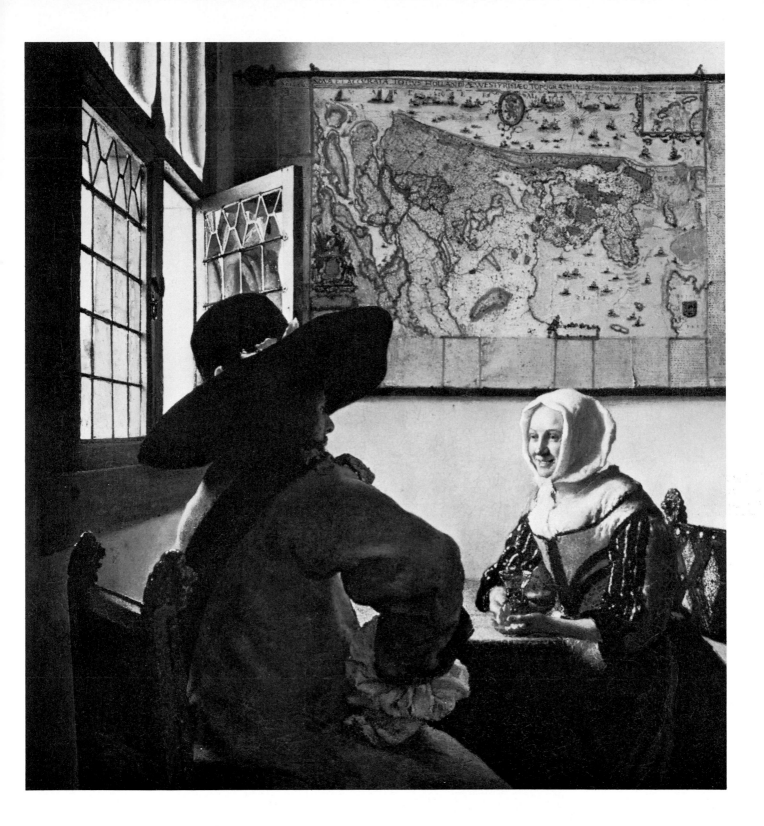

from the de Brais collection, Paris. It was first identified as by Vermeer in 1858 by Gustav Waagen, eminent director of the Berlin Gallery, an attribution confirmed by Thoré-Bürger in 1859. Previously it had masqueraded under attributions as widely diverse as Rembrandt, Govaert Flinck and Pieter de Hoogh.

(*above*)
9 *Interior with a Soldier and a Girl Laughing*
NEW YORK, Frick Collection. Canvas 50.5 × 46 cm. Unsigned

Almost certainly in the 1696 sale as lot 11, the picture remained unknown until 1866 when Thoré-Bürger saw it in the collection of Léopold Double, Paris. Double had bought it at an un-specified London sale, attributed to Pieter de Hoogh. It was in the Double sale, Paris, 1881, when it was sold for the enormous sum of 88,000 francs, and subsequently in the Samuel Joseph collection, London. Mrs. Joseph sold it to Knoedler, from whom Henry Clay Frick bought it in 1911.

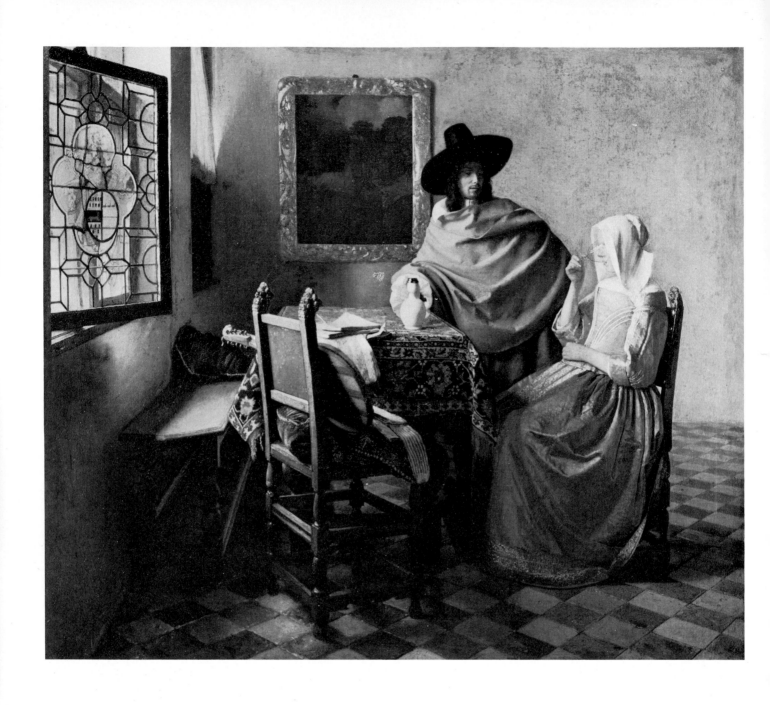

10 *Interior with a Gentleman and a Young Woman with a Wineglass*
BERLIN-DAHLEM, Staatliche Gemäldegalerie. Canvas 65 × 77 cm. Unsigned

First recorded as in the collection of Jan van Loon at Delft and in his sale on 18 July 1736, the picture then disappeared for over 150 years, until 1891, when it appeared as part of the collection of Lord Henry Francis Pelham Clinton Hope. Lord Henry sold his collection en bloc to Colnaghi and Wertheimer in 1898. The picture was then acquired by that most astute of museum curators, Wilhelm von Bode, for the then Kaiser Friedrich Museum in Berlin in 1901.

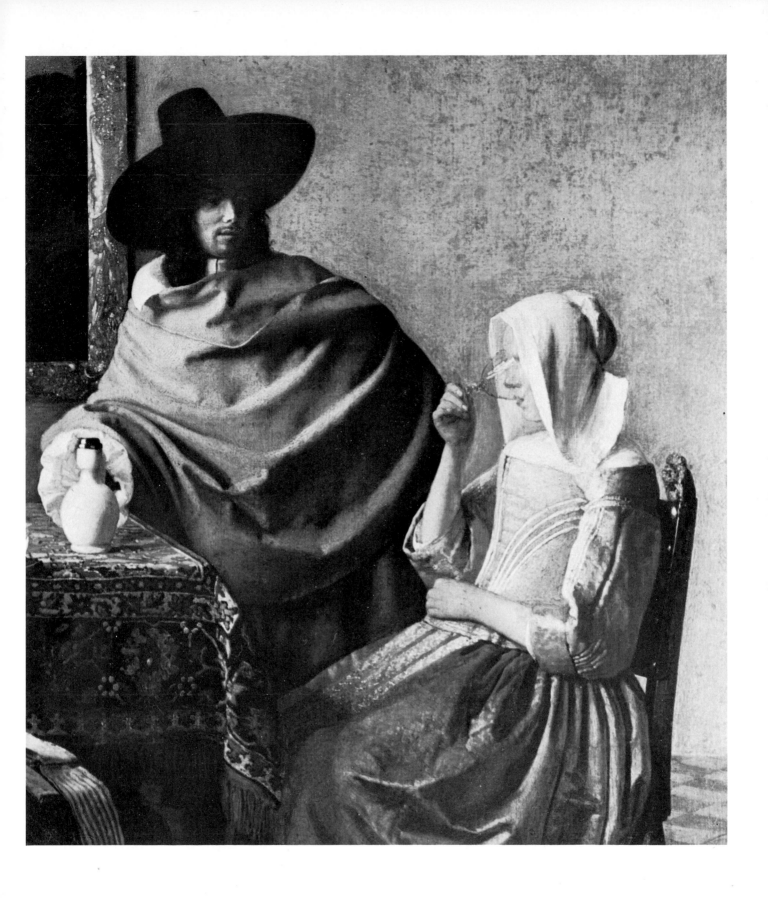

Interior with a Gentleman and a Young Woman with a Wineglass (detail)

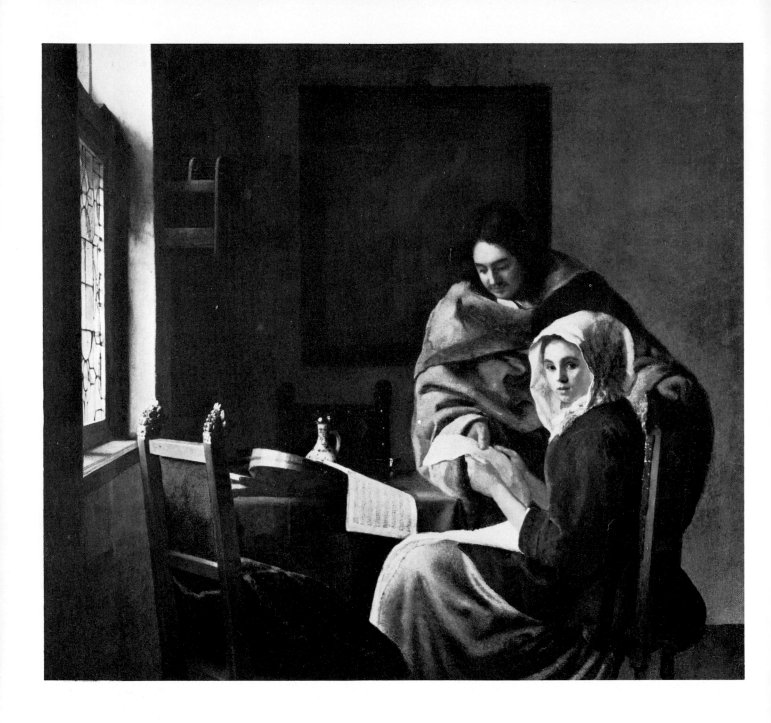

11 *Interior with a Girl Interrupted at her Music*
NEW YORK, Frick Collection. Canvas 39.3 × 44.4 cm. Unsigned

The picture already was attributed to Vermeer of Delft when it appeared in the Pieter Smeth
van Alpen sale in Amsterdam in 1810. It was sold again in the following year, reappearing at an
Amsterdam auction in 1820, and in 1853 was sold at Christie's, London, as from the collection of
Samuel Woodburn, making the very modest sum of £42. Passing into the noted collection of
Francis Gibson of Saffron Walden and then by descent to his daughter, Mrs. Lewis Fry of Bristol,
the picture was in the hands of the London dealers Lawrie and Co., who also managed the sale of
the London *Lady Standing at the Virginals* (Plate 33). Henry Clay Frick acquired the painting, the
first of the three Vermeers he was to own, through Knoedler in 1901. Modern scholarship has seen
fit to doubt the authenticity of the *Girl Interrupted at her Music* in spite of its being one of Vermeer's
most subtle compositions. The picture's history in the salerooms proves at least that it is not a
nineteenth or twentieth century fabrication. It is in a rubbed condition and has been described as
overpainted.

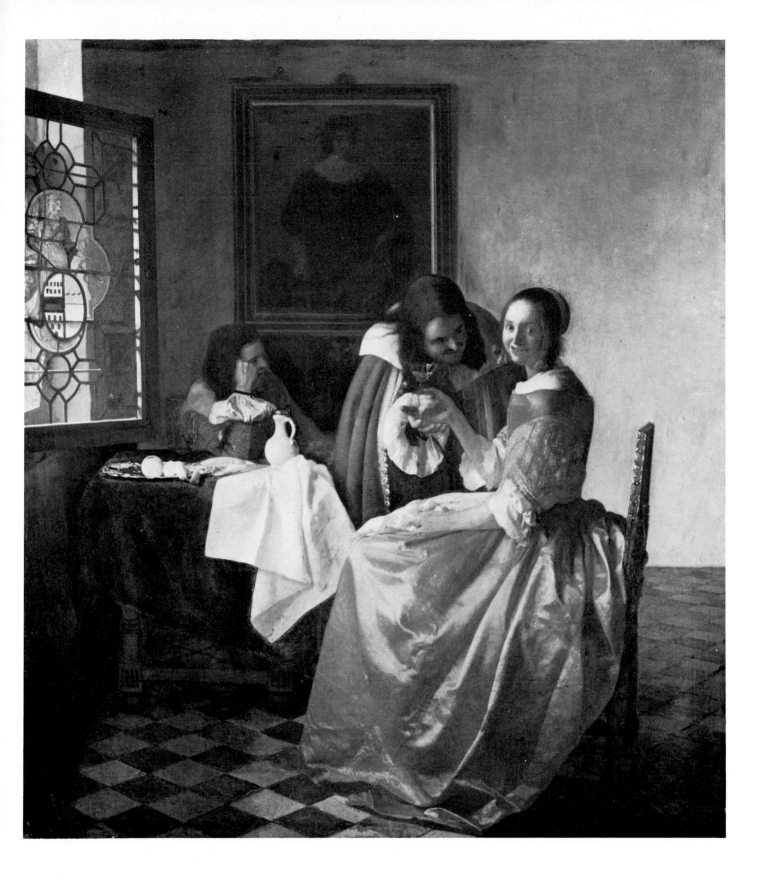

12 *Interior with Two Gentlemen and a Girl with a Wineglass*
BRUNSWICK, Herzog Anton-Ulrich Museum. Canvas 78 × 67 cm. Signed on the wall by the window:
I V Meer

Possibly lot 9 in the 1696 sale, although there is a large element of doubt, the picture was recorded
in the collection of Anton Ulrich, Duke of Brunswick-Wolfenbüttel (1633–1714), as early as 1710,
when it was described as being by 'von der Mair'. It has remained in the Ducal Gallery at Brunswick ever since, although in 1935 an unsuccessful attempt was made to sell it from the collection.
The picture was last restored in 1913. The background appears to have been overpainted but
otherwise the painting is in good condition.

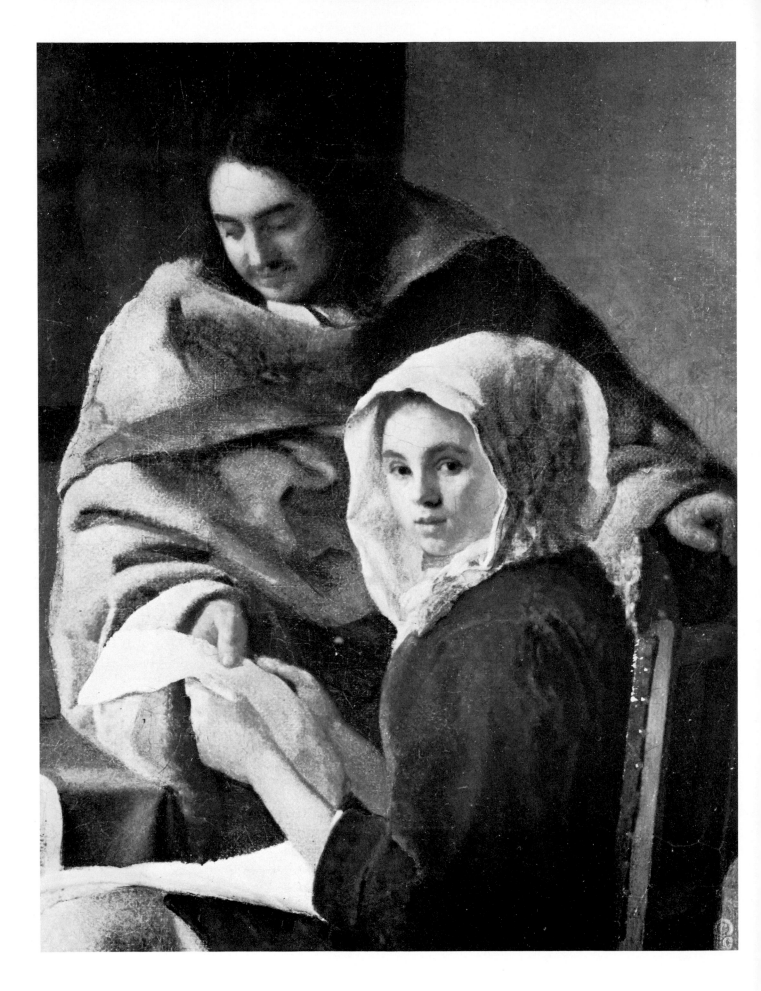

Interior with a Girl Interrupted at her Music (detail) Plate 11

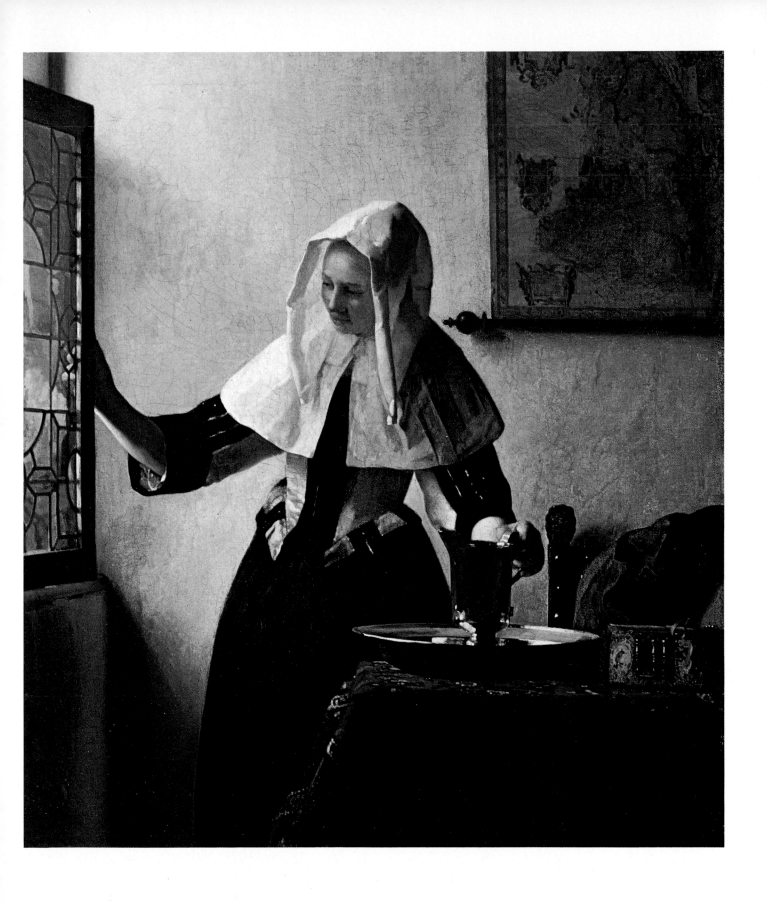

III *Interior with a Girl at a Window with a Jug* (Plate 13)
New York, Metropolitan Museum of Art (Bequest of Henry G. Marquand)

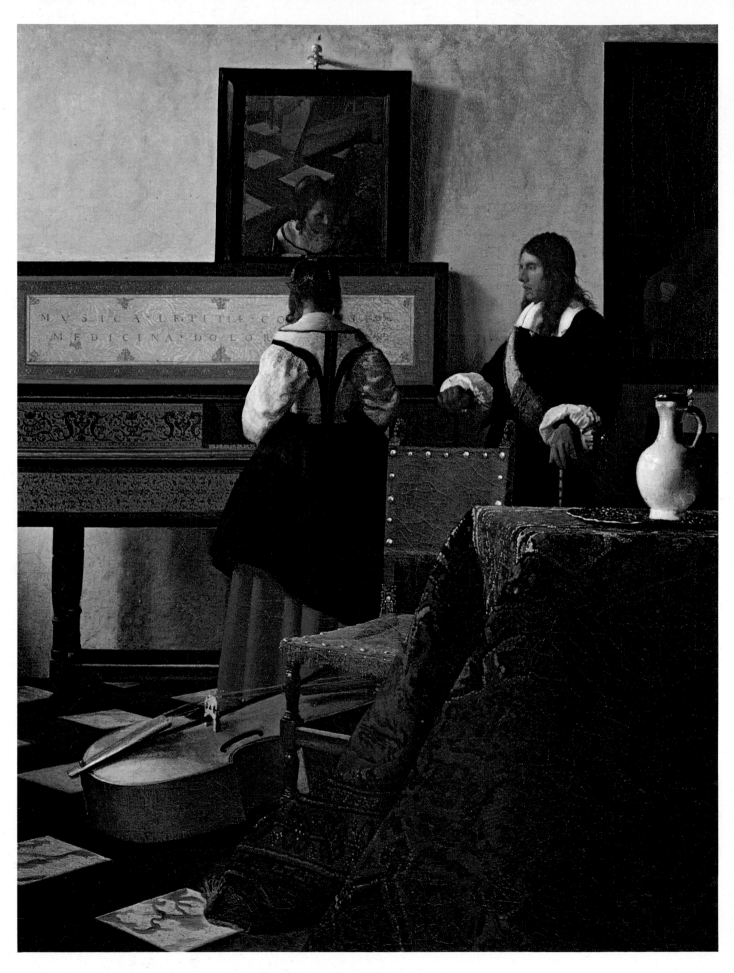

IV *Interior with a Lady at the Virginals with a Gentleman* (*The Music Lesson*) (Plate 14, detail)
Windsor Castle, Royal Collection (Reproduced by Gracious Permission of Her Majesty the Queen)

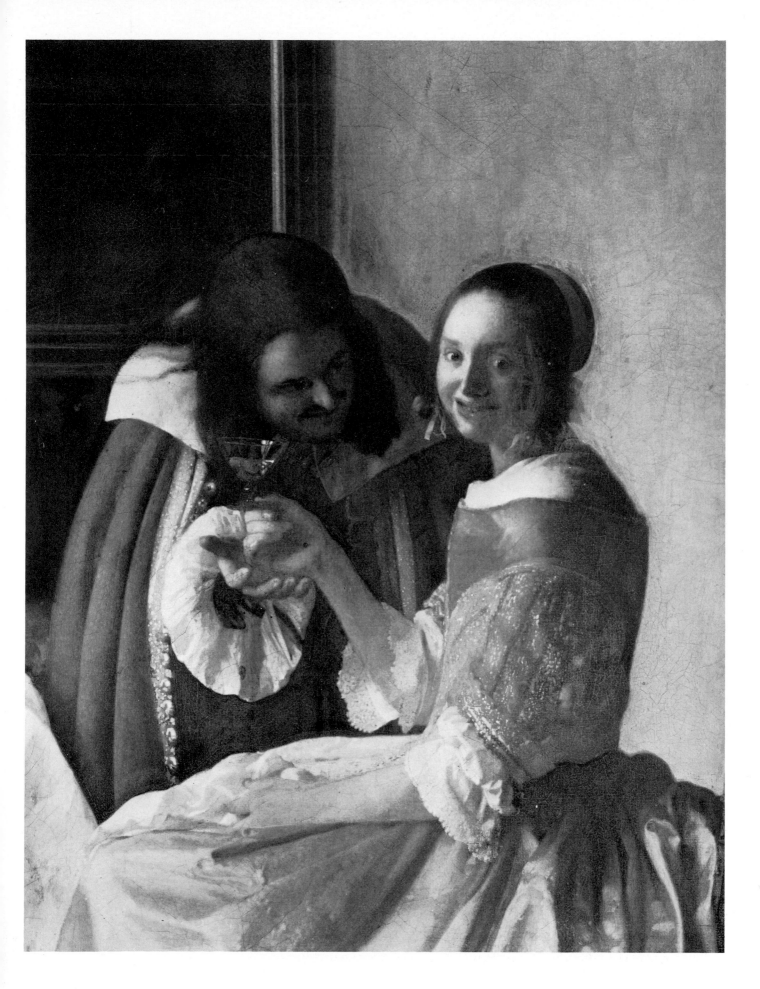

Interior with Two Gentlemen and a Girl with a Wineglass (detail) Plate 12

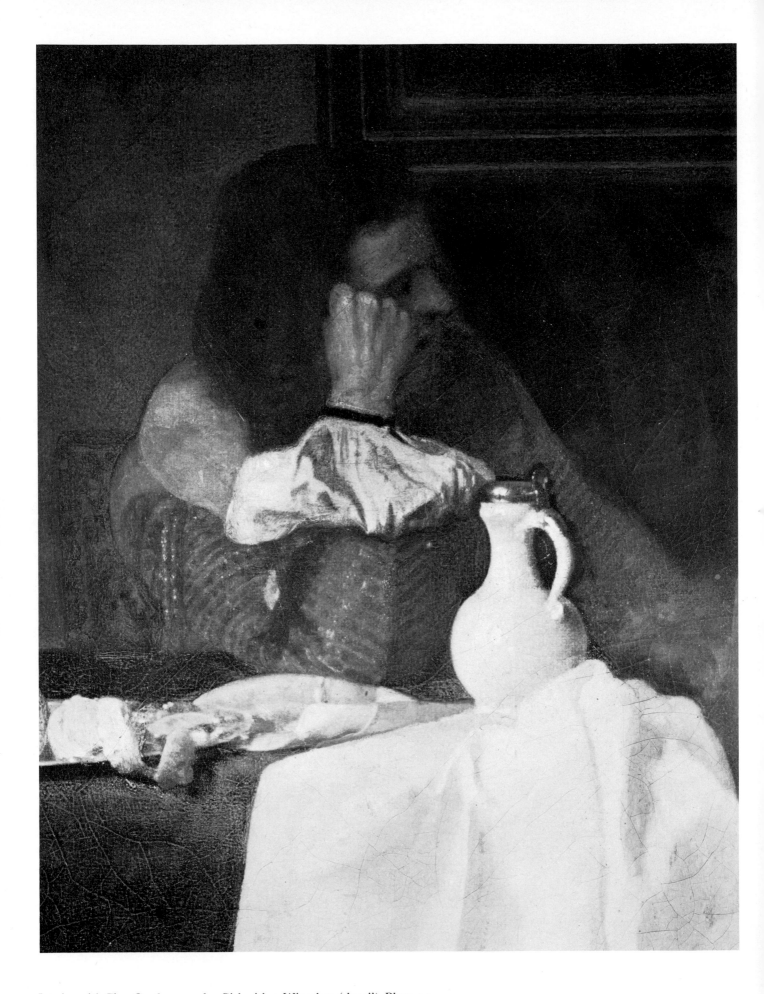

Interior with Two Gentlemen and a Girl with a Wineglass (detail) Plate 12

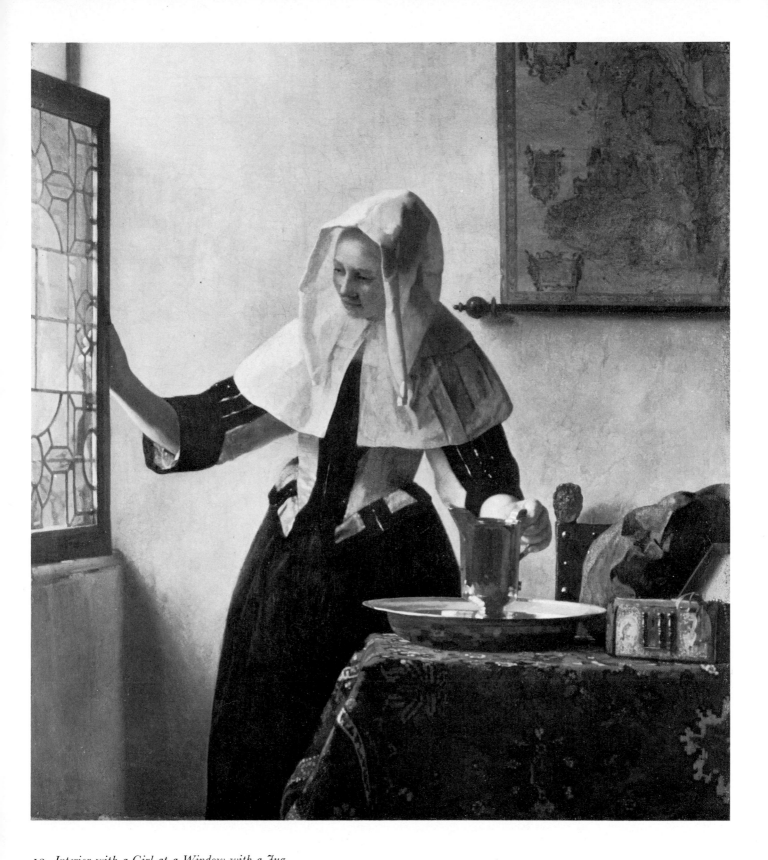

13 *Interior with a Girl at a Window with a Jug*
NEW YORK, Metropolitan Museum of Art (Bequest of Henry Marquand). Canvas 44 × 39 cm. Unsigned

The picture was first recorded at Hatley Park in Cambridgeshire in 1838, in the collection of
Robert Vernon, who lent it to the British Institution in that year, attributed to Metsu. It was
bought by Colnaghi's for £404 and 5 shillings in the Vernon sale, London, Christie's, 21 April 1877,
still ascribed it to Metsu, and soon after was sold for 600 guineas to Lord Powerscourt, who lent
it to the Royal Academy Old Master Exhibition in 1878 as by Vermeer of Delft. The picture was
unknown to Thoré-Bürger, who had died in 1869, and it would be interesting to know who made
the attribution to Vermeer between 1877 and 1878. This correct attribution, however, cannot have
been taken seriously, for in 1887 Henry Marquand acquired it from Charles Pillet, Paris, for $800,
attributed to Pieter de Hoogh. Marquand gave the picture to the Metropolitan Museum in 1888.

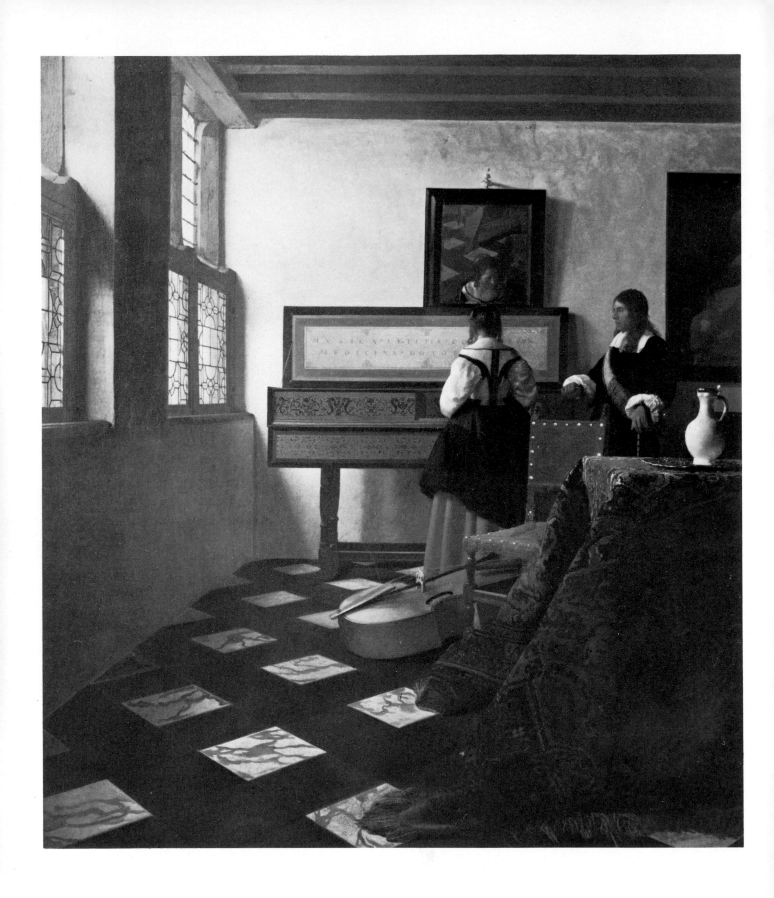

14 *Interior with a Lady at the Virginals with a Gentleman* (*The Music Lesson*)
WINDSOR CASTLE, Royal Collection (reproduced by Gracious Permission of Her Majesty the Queen).
Canvas 73.6 × 64 cm. Signed on the picture frame at the right: I V Meer

Almost certainly lot 6 in the 1696 sale, the picture also might have been in an Amsterdam sale in
1714, but its provenance cannot be identified positively until it was bought from the collection of
the Italian artist Giovanni Antonio Pellegrini (1675–1741) by Consul Smith. The latter sold the
picture to George III in 1762 with an attribution to Frans van Mieris; the Vermeer signature was
ignored.

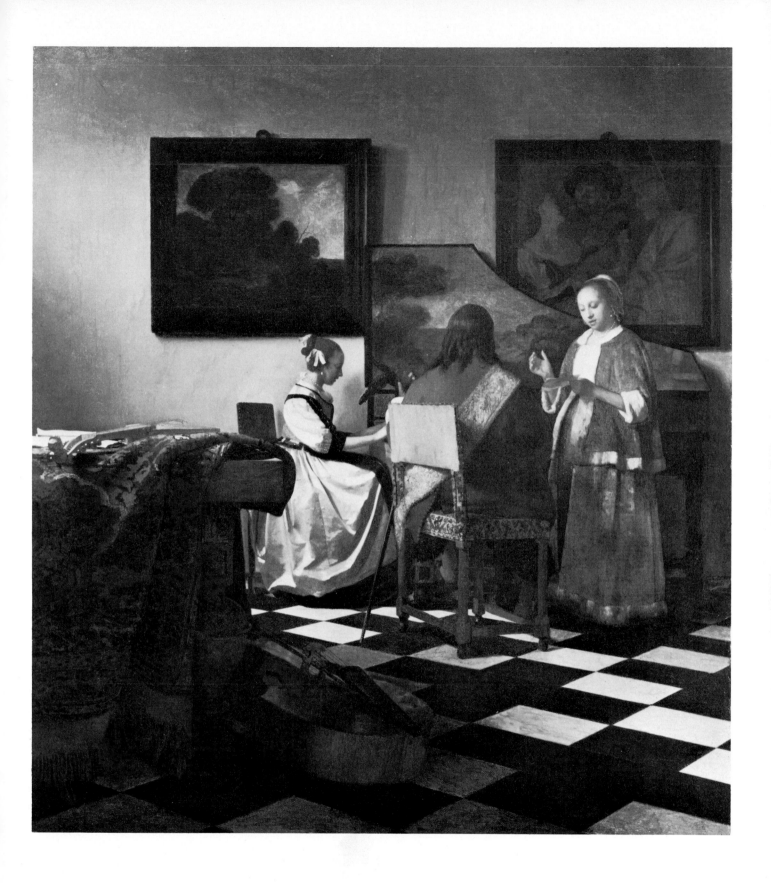

15 *Interior with Two Ladies and a Gentleman Making Music* (*The Concert*)
BOSTON, Isabella Stewart Gardner Museum. Canvas 71 × 63 cm. Unsigned

Described as by Vermeer of Delft when sold in Amsterdam in 1780, *The Concert* reappeared in a
Paris sale in 1804 and was then at Christie's, London, in 1860, when it made the ridiculously low
price of £21. Nine years later when the picture was sold in Paris the price had risen to 5100
francs, presumably following Thoré-Bürger's article of 1866. The picture must have been acquired
by Thoré-Bürger at the sale or soon after as it appeared in his posthumous sale—he died in 1869—
which did not take place until 1892. The picture was purchased by Robert for Mrs. Gardner at the
Thoré sale.

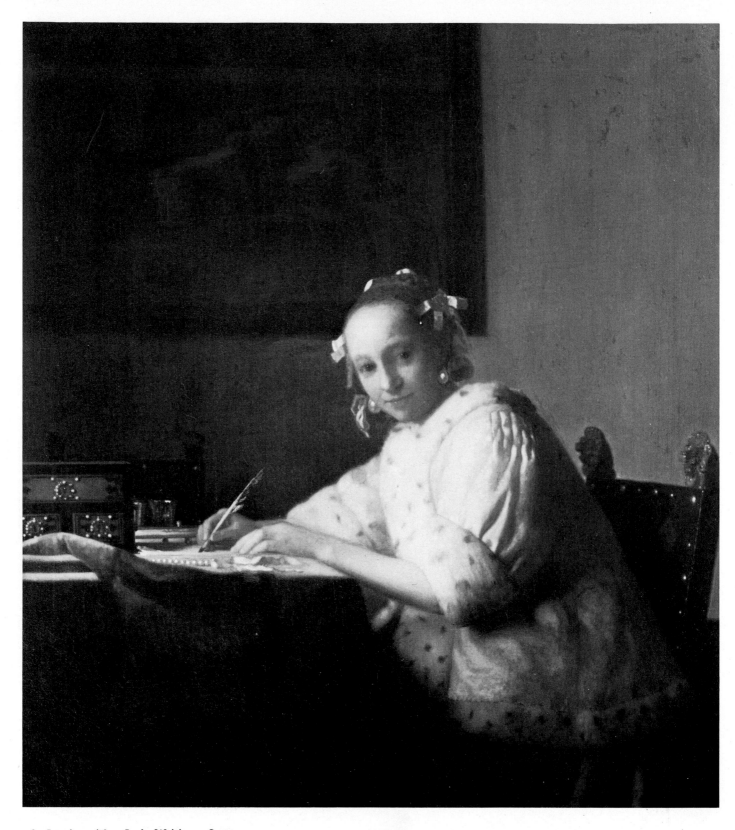

16 *Interior with a Lady Writing a Letter*
WASHINGTON, National Gallery of Art (Gift of H. W. and H. Havemeyer). Canvas 45 × 39.9 cm.
Signed on the bottom of the frame of the picture on the wall: IVMeer

The picture may have been in the 1696 sale as lot 35, although the description is rather vague. It
was not recorded again until its appearance in a Rotterdam sale in 1816, was sold a second time in
Rotterdam in 1825 and again, two years later, in Amsterdam. The picture then appeared in Brussels
in 1837 as from the collection of Count F. de Robiano, and was on the Paris art market in 1907,
passing, in the following year, into the Pierpont Morgan collection in New York. It was acquired
from Knoedler by Lady Oakes of Nassau, the Bahamas, who, in 1958, sold it back to Knoedler,
who, in turn, sold it to Mrs. Horace Havemeyer of New York. It was given finally to the National
Gallery in Washington in 1962 by Henry Waldron Havemeyer and Horace Havemeyer Jr. in
memory of their father Horace Havemeyer.

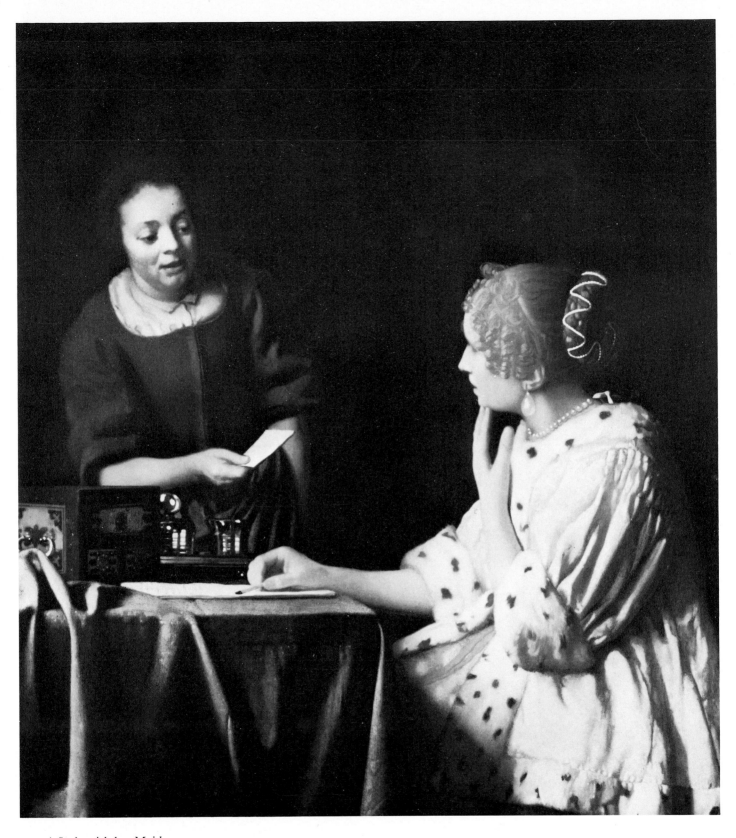

17 *A Lady with her Maid*
NEW YORK, Frick Collection. Canvas 92 × 78.7 cm. Unsigned

This picture was particularly appreciated in nineteenth century France. Probably in the 1696 sale as lot 7, although the reference could have been to the Amsterdam *Lady with her Maid* (Plate 29), it may have been sold in Amsterdam in 1738, although the description in the catalogue is, again, ambiguous. It ultimately formed part of the collection of the duchesse de Berri, in whose 1837 sale it made 415 francs, and, by 1859, had found its way into the Dufour collection, Marseilles, where Thoré-Bürger must have seen it. Sold in the E. Secrétan sale, Paris, 1889, for the enormous sum of 75,000 francs, it was then in the Paulovstov collection, St. Petersburg, and on the London art market by 1905. Hofstede de Groot noted it in the collection of James Simon, Berlin, who is believed to have paid 325,000 marks for it. The picture was acquired by Frick from Duveen in 1919.

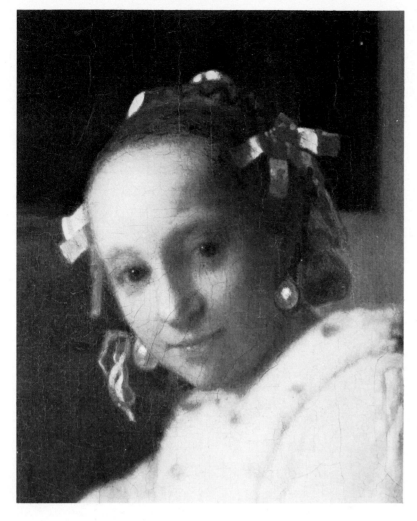

Interior with a Lady Writing a Letter (detail) Plate 16

(*opposite: top*)
18 *Portrait of a Young Woman*
NEW YORK, Private Collection. Canvas 44.5 × 40 cm. Signed upper left: I Meer

Possibly but by no means certainly in the 1696 sale as lot 38 or even lots 39 or 40, the picture may also have been sold in Rotterdam in 1816 as the dimensions correspond but the description is vague. Acquired by Prince Auguste d'Arenberg before 1829, it remained in the Arenberg collection, firstly in,Brussels and later at the Schloss Meppen in Germany, until 1955, the year it was acquired by the present owners. While in the Arenberg collection the picture was rarely seen, but Thoré-Bürger devoted a memorable passage to it. 'Her face has a melancholy finesse which forces one to look at this woman with a mysterious sympathy. It makes one think of the silent images evoked by Rembrandt and, curiously enough, of certain of Correggio's faces, and even, with the exception of the difference of the beauty of the type, of the prestigious Mona Lisa of Leonardo.' The picture has been described as being in a damaged condition, but, as with many other pictures by Vermeer, this could have resulted from changes in the chemical composition of the paint.

(*opposite: bottom*)
19 *Head of a Girl with a Pearl Earring*
THE HAGUE, Mauritshuis. Canvas 46.5 × 40 cm. Signed upper left: I Meer

This picture is usually thought to have been in the 1696 sale but like the painting of a similar subject in a New York private collection (Plate 18), it could have been any one of three lots, or, perhaps, may not have been in the sale at all. It was sold at auction in The Hague from the Braam collection in 1882 when it was bought by A. A. des Tombe for the ridiculous sum of two and one-half florins. Thus the fame of the picture belongs entirely in the twentieth century. It was bequeathed by des Tombe to the Mauritshuis in 1903. The picture is not in good condition, but this appears to have been caused by changes in the chemistry of the paint rather than later damage.

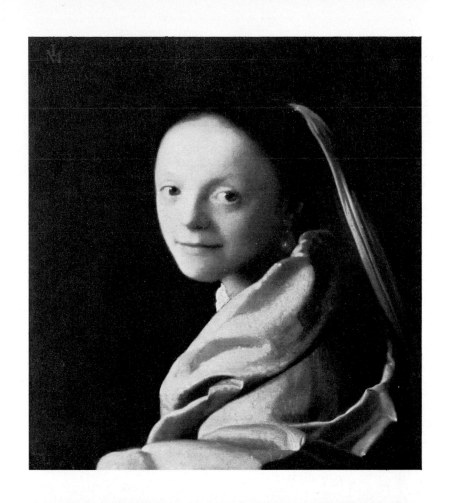

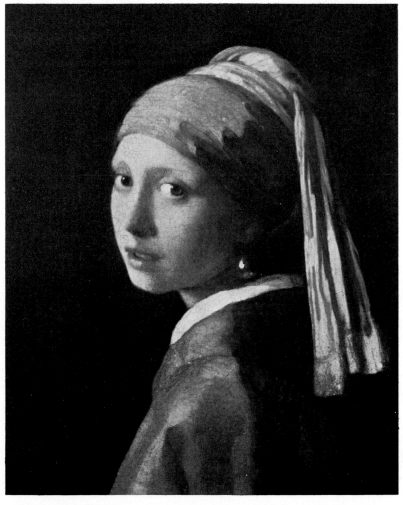

45

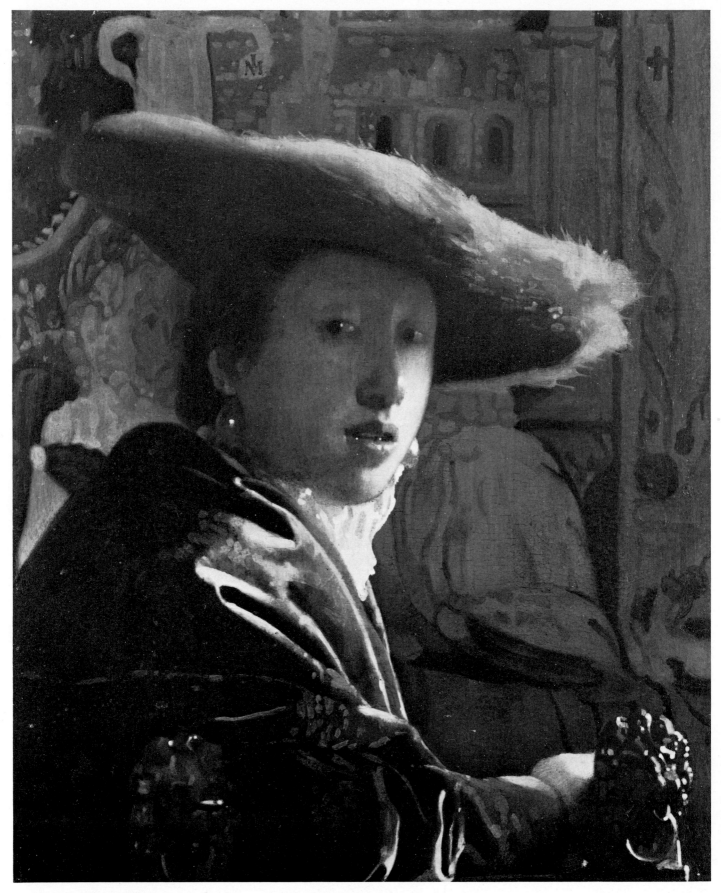

20 *The Girl in a Red Hat*
WASHINGTON, National Gallery of Art (Andrew W. Mellon Collection). Panel 23 × 18 cm. Signed in monogram upper left: VM

The picture was first recorded in 1822 at the La Fontaine sale, Paris, attributed, significantly, to 'Van der Meer de Delft', and was later owned by Baron Atthalin, Colmar. It was given to the Gallery by A. Mellon in 1937.

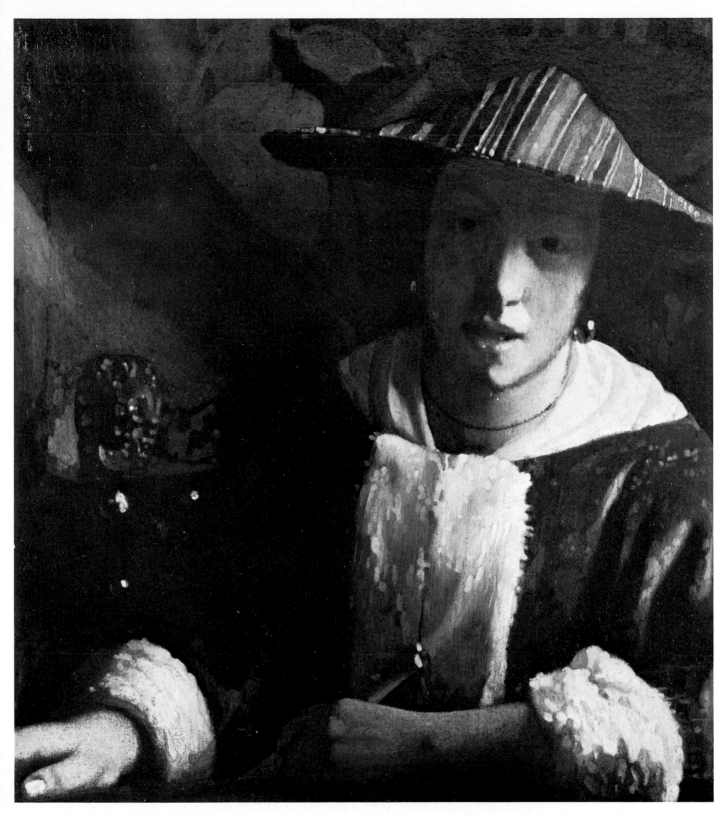

21 *The Girl with a Flute*
WASHINGTON, National Gallery of Art (Widener Collection). Panel 20 × 18 cm. Unsigned

The early history of this controversial picture is obscure. United with its so-called pendant in Washington only in 1942, *The Girl with a Flute* was recorded first in the Grez van Boxtel collection at 's Hertogenbosch and then was transferred to Brussels, where it formed part of the de Grez collection. The picture was discovered by Bredius, who exhibited it at the Mauritshuis in 1906/07, and it then became part of the August Janssen collection, Amsterdam. Later it passed from Goudstikker, Amsterdam, to Knoedler, New York, who sold it to Joseph Widener of Elkins Park, Philadelphia, who, in turn, gave it to Washington in 1942 as part of the group of pictures which formed the basis of the newly founded National Gallery. Recent scholarship has cast doubts on the authenticity of this masterpiece because it seems untypical of Vermeer's style. It is the direct approach to the subject which is unusual.

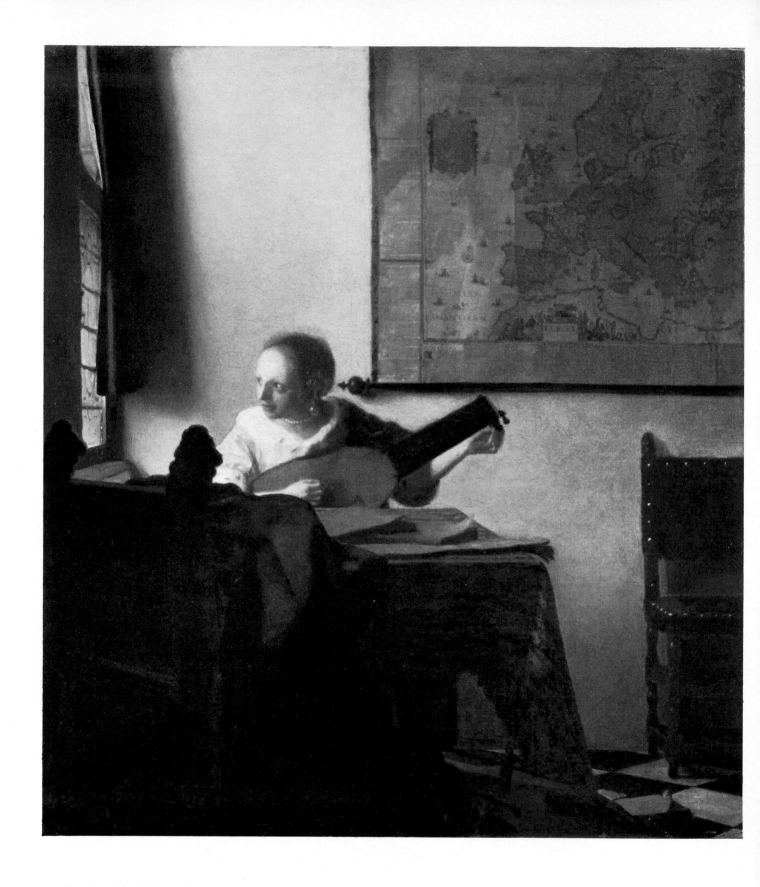

22 *Interior with a Woman Playing the Lute*
NEW YORK, Metropolitan Museum of Art (Bequest of Collis P. Huntington). Canvas 52 × 46 cm.
Unsigned

This picture seems to have been unknown to both Thoré-Bürger and Hofstede de Groot. Sold
in Amsterdam in 1817 with an attribution to Vermeer, it was subsequently in England, where it was
acquired from an unspecified collection by Collis P. Huntington, who bequeathed it to the
Metropolitan Museum in 1897. The picture is in poor condition and badly rubbed in the shadows,
although enough is left to make it obvious that it is by Vermeer. Doubts, however, have been cast
recently by Blankert.

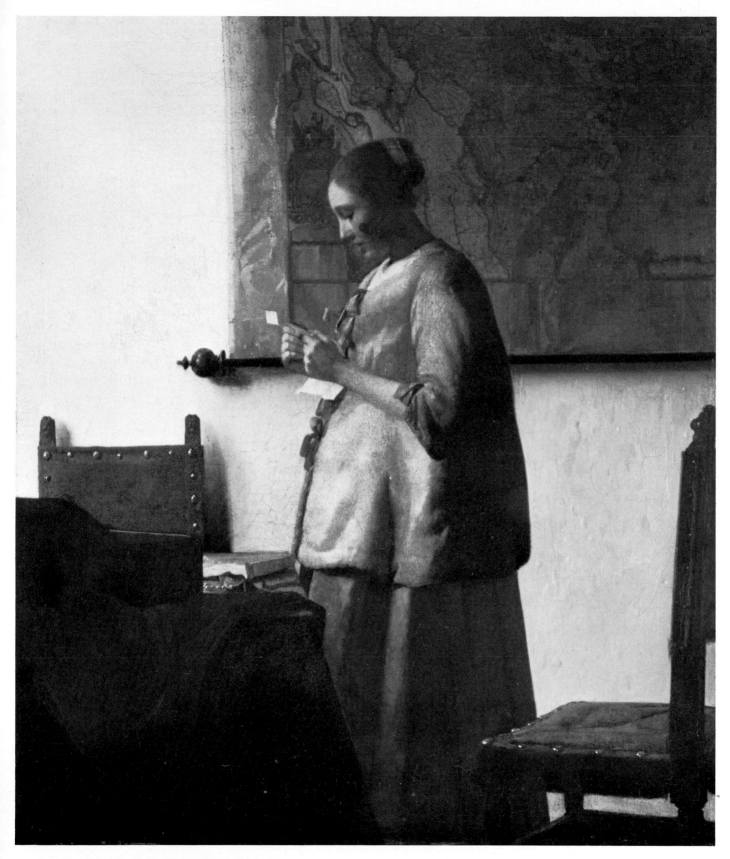

23 *Interior with a Lady Reading a Letter*
AMSTERDAM, Rijksmuseum. Canvas 46.5 × 39 cm. Unsigned

The picture was sold for 110 florins in the van der Lip sale, Amsterdam, 14 June 1712, although Hofstede de Groot expressed the view that the description could apply equally well to the Dresden *Interior with a Girl Reading a Letter* (Plate 8). Repeatedly sold in Amsterdam in 1772, 1791, 1793 and 1801, each time for a slightly higher price, it was in the Paillet sale, 1809, Paris, when it made 200 francs. When the picture was in the Lapéyrière sale, Paris, 1825, however, there was a startling increase in its price to 2060 francs. Subsequently it was owned by van der Hoop, who bequeathed it in 1854 to the city of Amsterdam. It was placed on permanent loan to the Rijksmuseum in 1885.

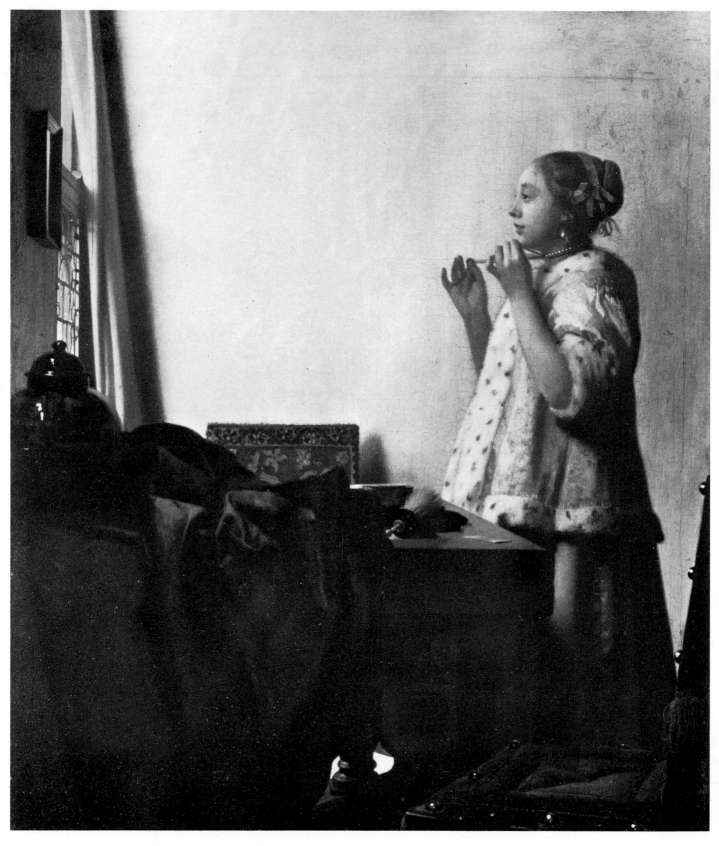

24 *Interior with a Young Woman with a Pearl Necklace*
BERLIN-DAHLEM, Staatliche Gemäldegalerie. Canvas 55 × 45 cm. Signed on the table: JvMeer

Quite possibly in the 1696 sale as lot 36, although described as a young woman *adorning* herself, the picture disappeared from view until 6 September 1809 when it made 55 florins in an Amsterdam sale and half a century later was sold again in Amsterdam, by which time the price had risen to 111 florins. The picture was acquired by Thoré-Bürger from the Henry Grevedon collection c. 1860. It is not quite certain whether Thoré-Bürger parted with this picture in his lifetime, but by 1874 it was certainly in the Suermondt collection at Aix-la-Chapelle, from whom it was acquired in that year by the then Kaiser Friedrich Museum, Berlin.

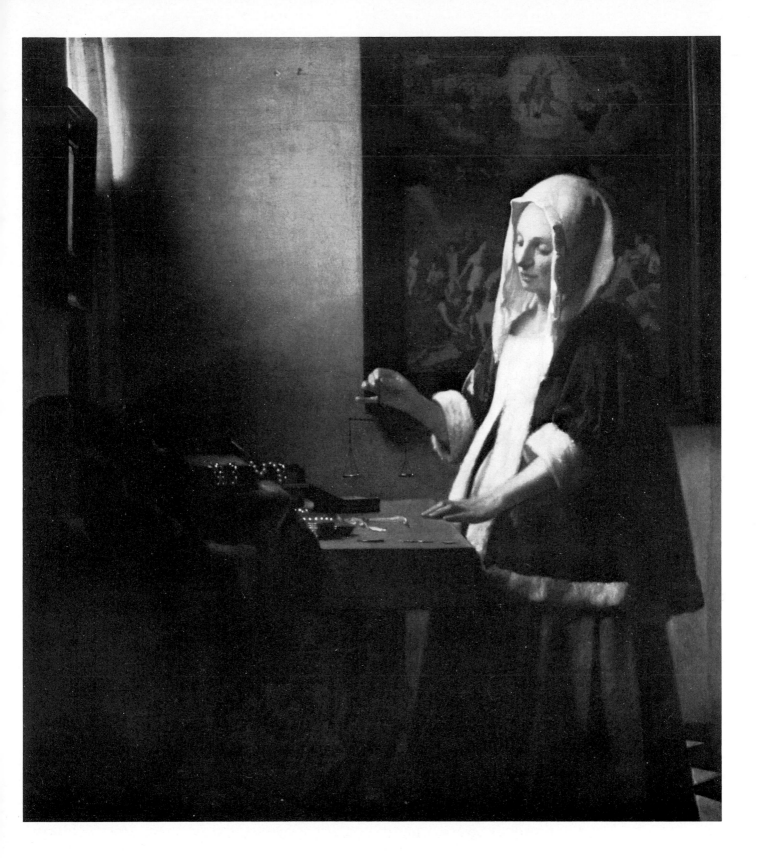

25 *Interior with a Woman Weighing Gold*
WASHINGTON, National Gallery of Art (Widener Collection). Canvas 42.5 × 38 cm.
Unsigned

Almost certainly lot 1 in the 1696 sale and again described as a 'gold weigher' when resold in
Amsterdam in 1701, the picture was later in the collection of Maximilian I Joseph, King of
Bavaria, at Munich and was in his sale, Munich, 5 December 1826. It was then on the art market
both in Paris (1830) and London (1848) and afterwards in the Paris collection of the Comtesse
Ségur Perier and in the London collection of F. Lippmann. It was sold through Colnaghi to
Joseph P. Widener of Elkins Park, Philadelphia, who donated it as part of his foundation gift to the
National Gallery in 1942.

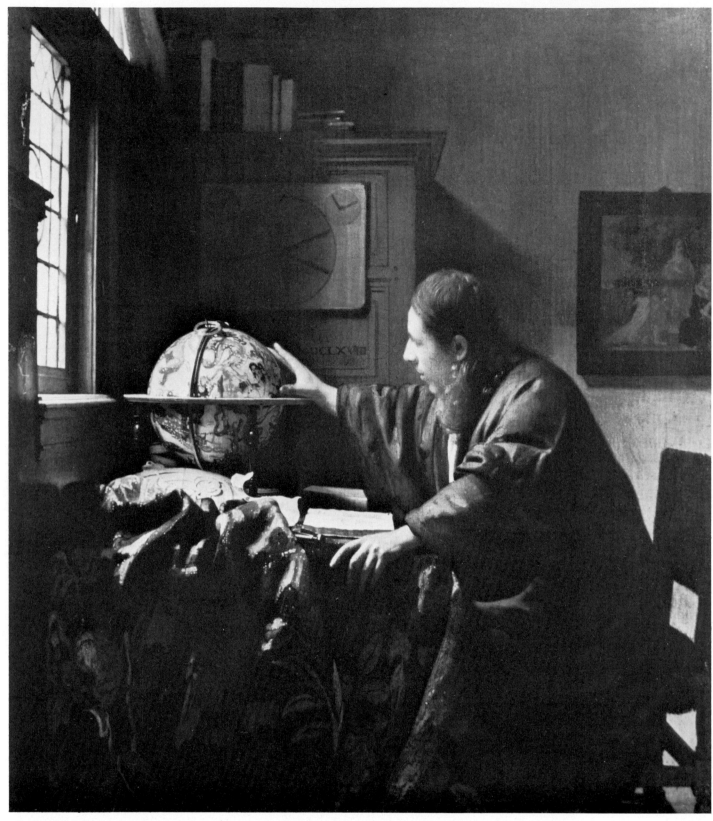

26 *Interior with an Astronomer*

PARIS, Private Collection. Canvas 51 × 45 cm. Signed and dated upper right: Meer MDCLXVIII [1668]

Throughout the numerous sales in the eighteenth century this picture appeared with its pendant, the Frankfurt *Geographer* (Plate 27). Both paintings were recorded first in Rotterdam in 1713 and then were sold repeatedly in Amsterdam in 1720, 1729 and 1778. By 1784 it was with the dealer Charles-Baptiste-Pierre Le Brun (1748–1814) (see fig. 8, p. 77). The picture was back in Amsterdam in 1797 when it was sold, this being the last time *The Astronomer* and *The Geographer* were together. *The Astronomer* was resold in Amsterdam in 1800 and is supposed to have been sold in London in 1863. It was then in the Léopold Double sale in Paris in 1881, as was the Frick *Soldier and a Girl Laughing* (Plate 9), when it made the considerable sum of 44,000 francs. From the collection of Baron Alphonse de Rothschild, Paris, the picture passed by descent to the present owner.

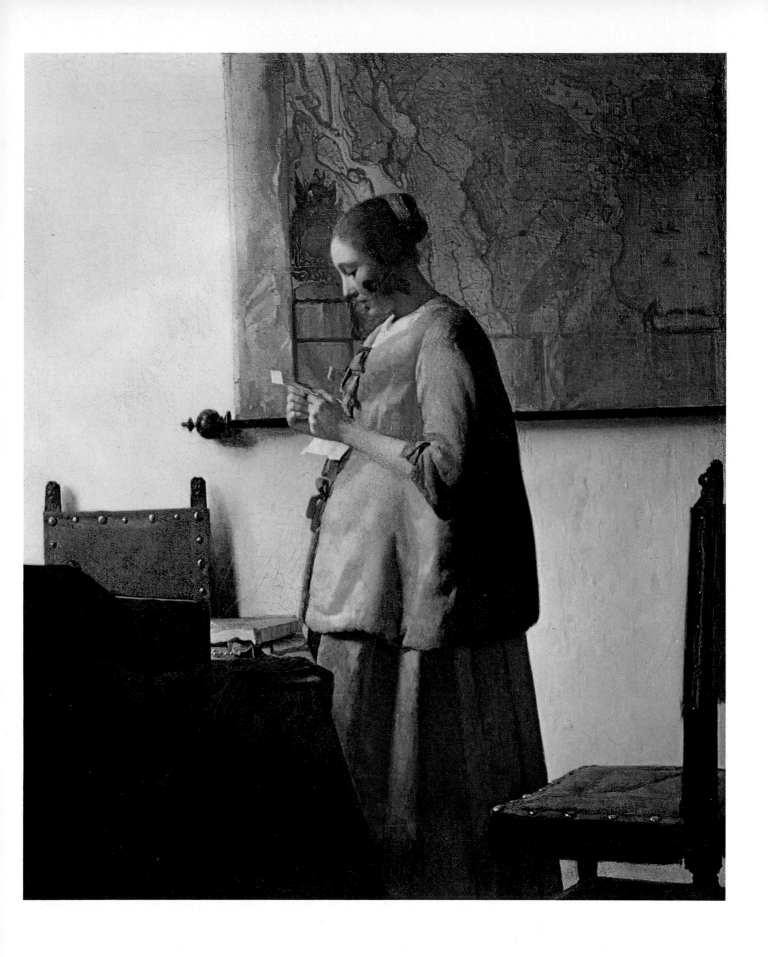

V *Interior with a Lady Reading a Letter* (Plate 23)
Amsterdam, Rijksmuseum

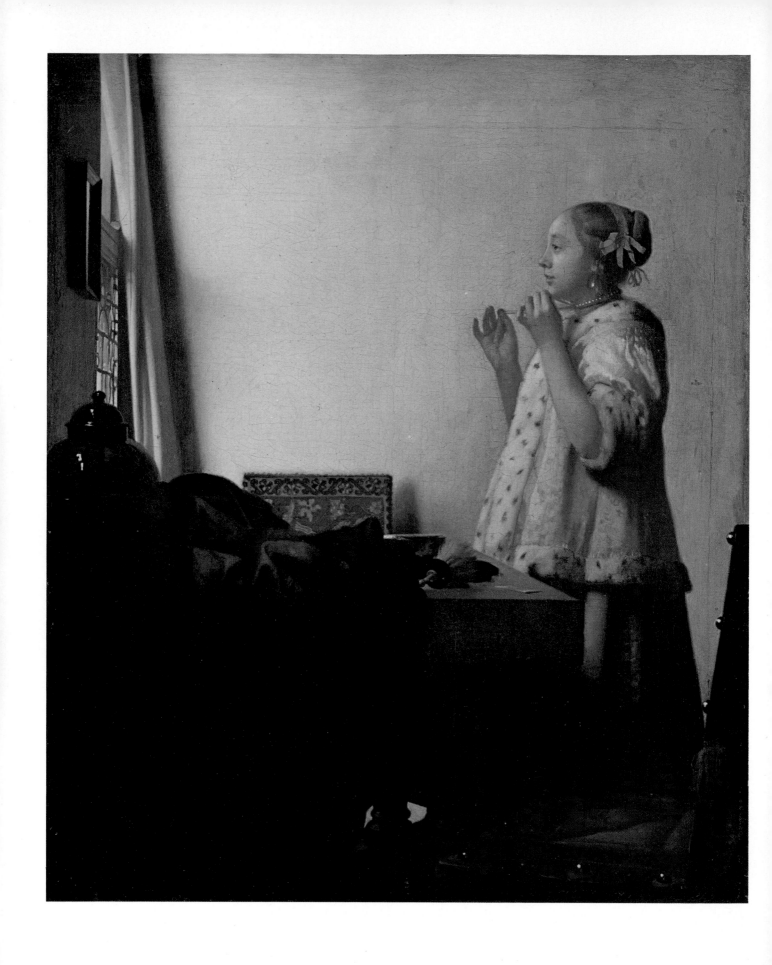

VI *Interior with a Young Woman with a Pearl Necklace* (Plate 24)
Berlin–Dahlem, Staatliche Gemäldegalerie

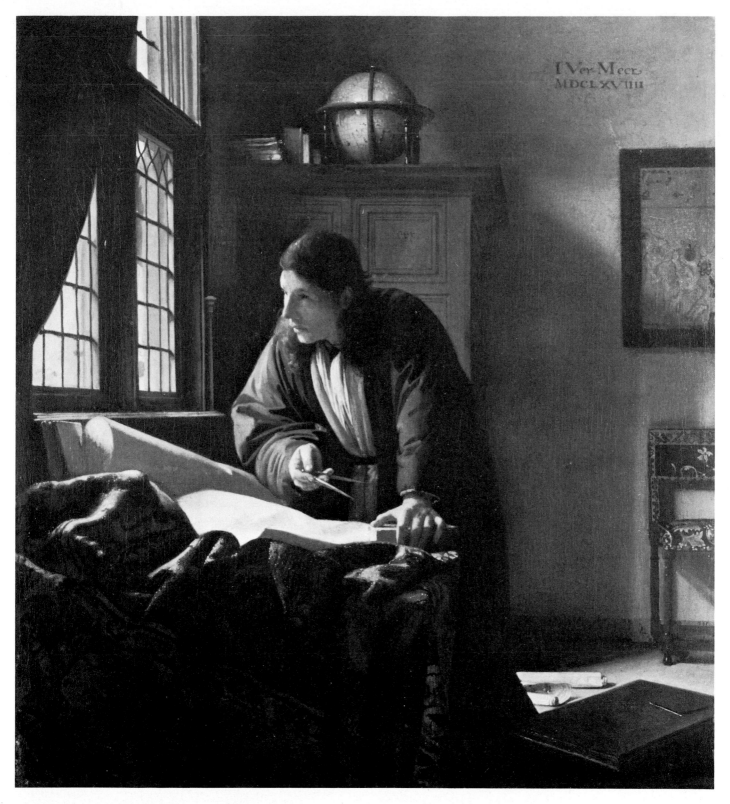

27 *Interior with a Geographer*

FRANKFURT-AM-MAIN, Städelsches Kunstinstitut. Canvas 53 × 46.6 cm. Signed and dated on the wall upper right: I Ver Meer MDCLXVIIII [1669]. Signed on the cupboard just above the geographer's head: Meer

To the naked eye the signature and date on the wall appear suspiciously modern. The picture's condition is far from perfect. The many changes of ownership in the eighteenth and nineteenth centuries easily could account for this. Throughout the numerous sales in the eighteenth century *The Geographer* appeared with its pendant *The Astronomer* (Plate 26). They were together for the last time in Amsterdam in 1797. By 1860 *The Geographer* was in the Dumont collection, Cambrai, and was in the Perier sale, Paris, 1872, making 7200 francs. This marked a turning point in rising prices for Vermeer's pictures following Thoré-Bürger's article of 1866. It was then sold in the Demidov sale, San Donato, Florence, in 1880 and by 1885 was with, first, Jos. Bosch, Vienna (see fig. 9, p. 77), and, later that year, with Sedelmeyer, Paris, from whom it was bought by the Frankfurter Kunstverein.

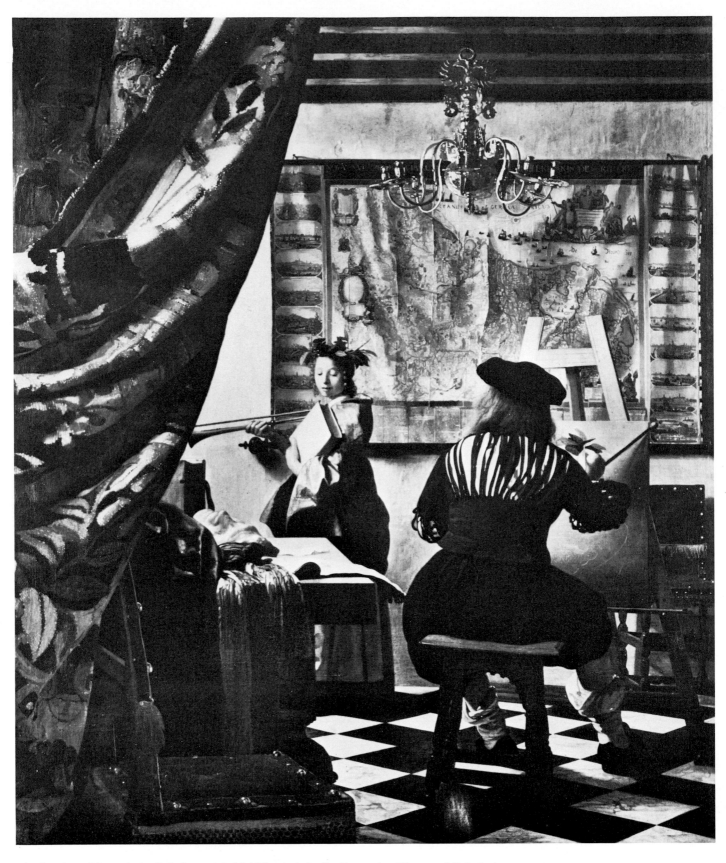

28 *Interior with an Artist Painting a Model* (*The Artist's Studio* or *An Allegory of Painting*)
VIENNA, Kunsthistorisches Museum. Canvas 120 × 100 cm. Unsigned

The Artist's Studio could well have been the painting given as security for a loan made to the
artist's widow immediately after his death, although the description is vague. Attempts have been
made to identify the picture as lot 3 in the 1696 sale. The picture's subsequent history is unknown
throughout the eighteenth century, and it appears to have been acquired in 1813 for 50 florins by
the graf von Czernin, Vienna, as by Pieter de Hoogh. It was removed from the Czernin

56

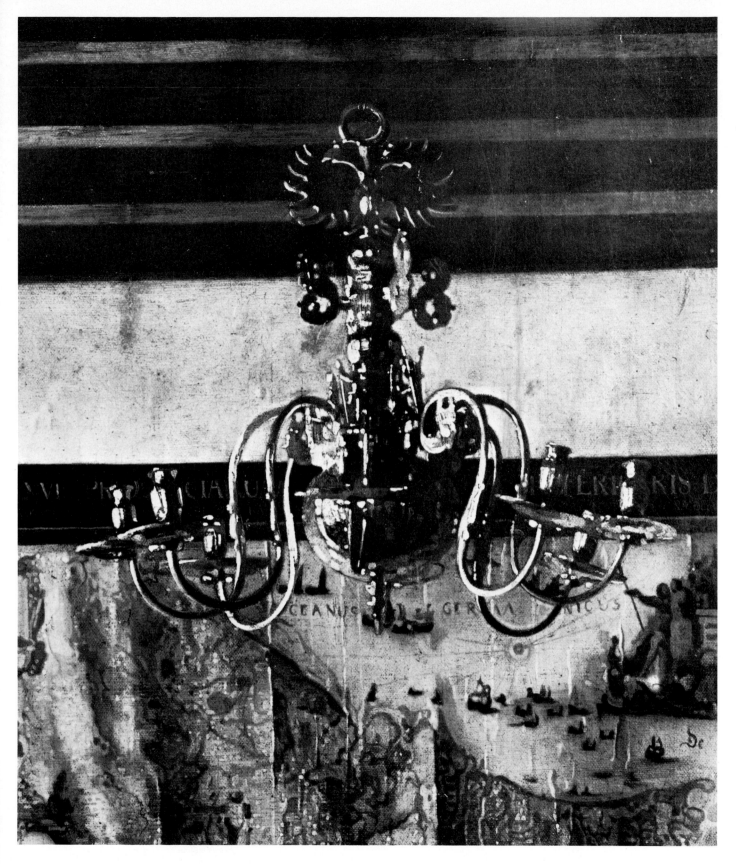

Interior with an Artist Painting a Model (detail)

collection c. 1939 by Adolf Hitler and taken to Berchtesgarten. Retrieved from an Austrian salt mine in 1945, the picture has been in the Kunsthistorisches Museum since 1946. *The Artist's Studio* was especially admired by Thoré-Bürger, who was the first to make the suggestion that the artist in the picture is Vermeer himself.

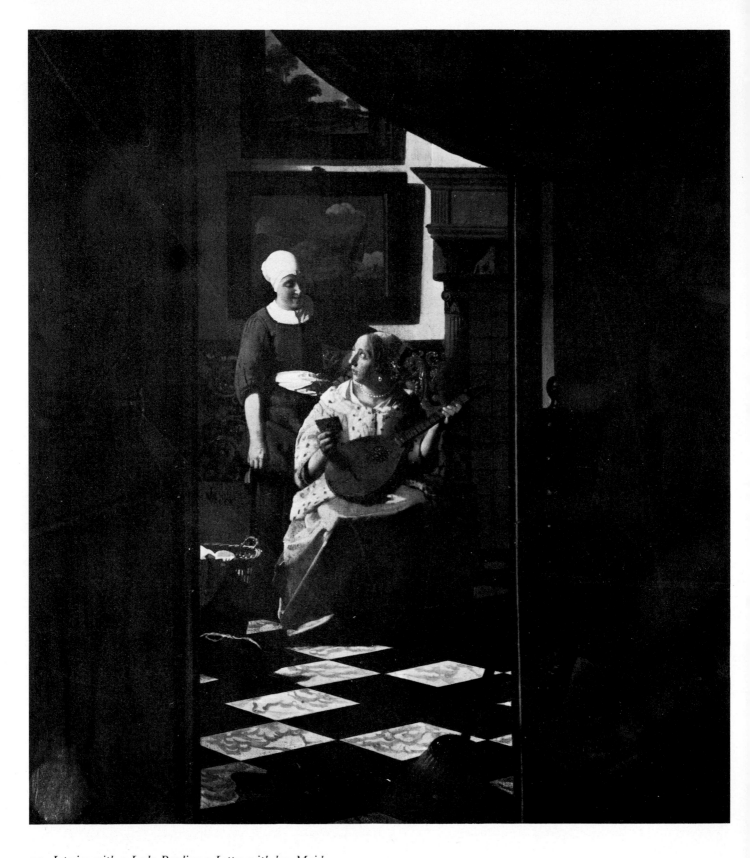

29 *Interior with a Lady Reading a Letter with her Maid*
AMSTERDAM, Rijksmuseum. Canvas 44 × 38.5 cm. Signed on the wall to the left of the maid:
IVMeer

The picture was possibly in the 1696 sale as lot 7, although the Frick painting of the same subject
(Plate 17) is also a possible candidate. In the nineteenth century it was in the collection of the van
Lennep family and, after 1850, in the collection of Messchert van Vollenhoven and in his sale,
Amsterdam, 29 March 1892. The picture was bought by the Rijksmuseum in the following year
with the aid of the Rembrandt Society. In 1971, while on exhibition at Brussels, the picture was
stolen and on its return was found to be seriously damaged. The restoration has been skilfully
done but no twentieth century restorer can approach Vermeer's clarity of vision.

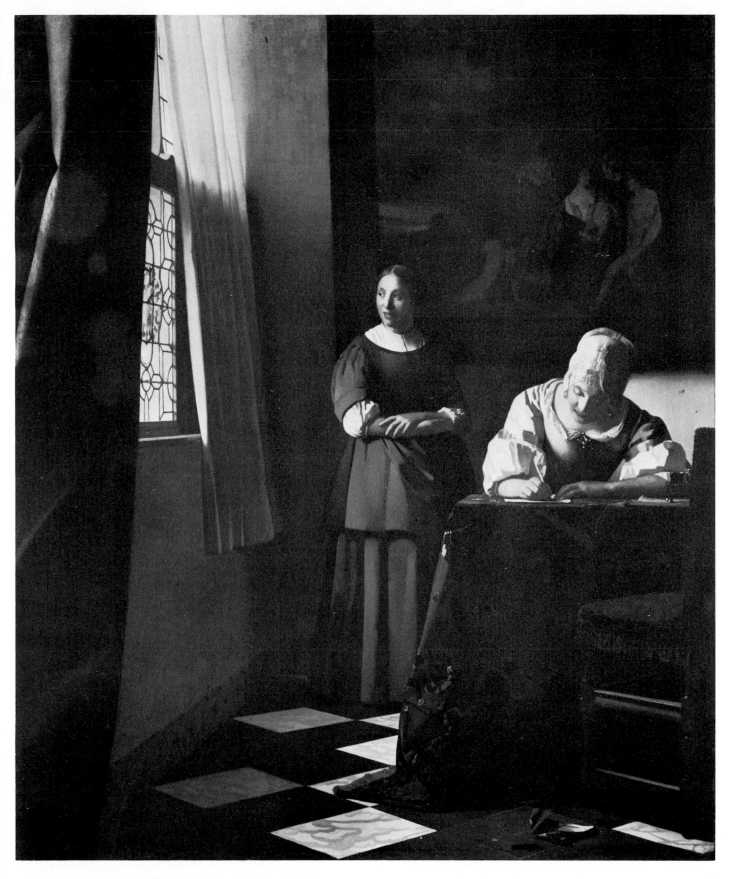

30 *Interior with a Lady Writing a Letter with her Maid*
BLESSINGTON, Russborough House, Collection of Sir Alfred Beit, Bt. Canvas 68.5 × 57.5 cm. Signed on the table cloth right: IVMeer

As the subject more or less corresponds to the contemporary description, this picture usually is identified, along with the Kenwood *Guitar Player* (Plate 32), as having been given towards payment of an outstanding bill by the artist's widow. It was not recorded again until its appearance in a Rotterdam sale in 1730. In 1761, when in the Hendrick van Slingelandt collection, The Hague,

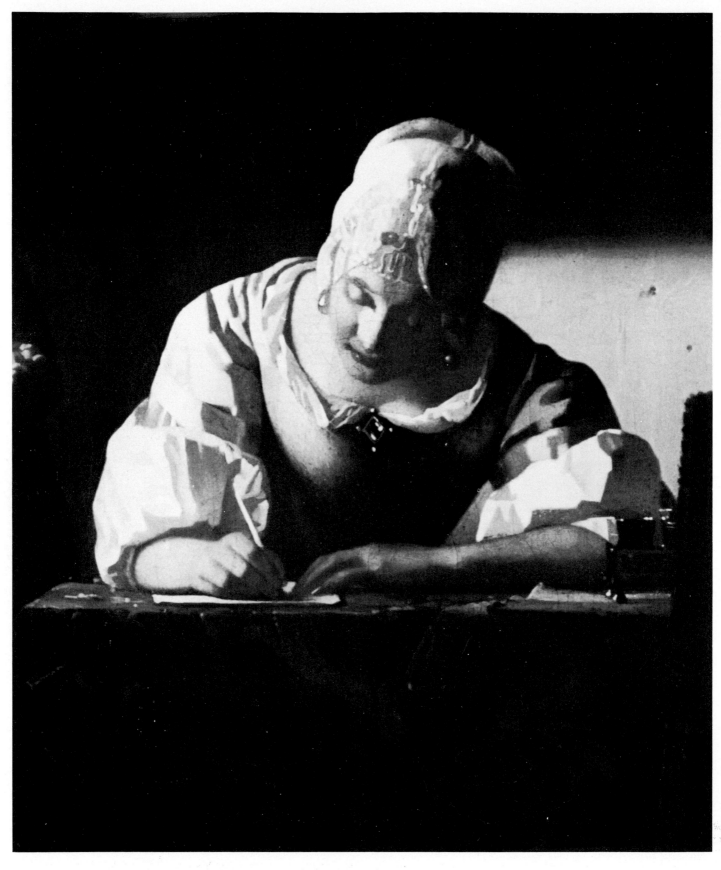

Interior with a Lady Writing a Letter with her Maid (detail) Plate 30

the picture was valued at 30 florins by the painter Aert Schouman. All trace of the painting is lost until the late nineteenth century, when it changed hands several times on the Paris art market. It was bought by Sir Alfred Beit, London, from whom it has descended to the present owner.

In 1974 the picture was stolen from Russborough and, following its safe return, was cleaned in the National Gallery of Ireland, Dublin.

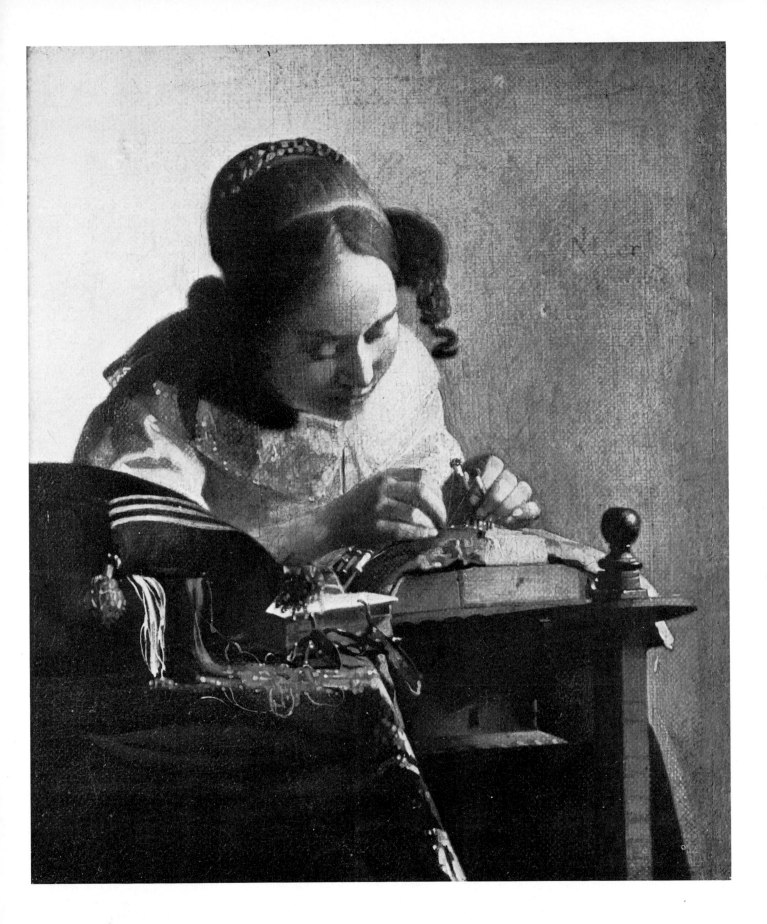

31 *The Lacemaker*
PARIS, Musée du Louvre. Canvas 24 × 21 cm. Signed on the wall upper right: JVMEER

In the 1696 sale as lot 12, *The Lacemaker* was not recorded again until the late eighteenth century from when it was sold surprisingly frequently, in 1778, 1810, 1813, 1815, 1817 and 1851. It was sold finally in Paris as from the D. Vis Blokhuyzen collection, Rotterdam, where Thoré-Bürger had seen it, and was acquired by the Louvre for 7500 francs soon after.

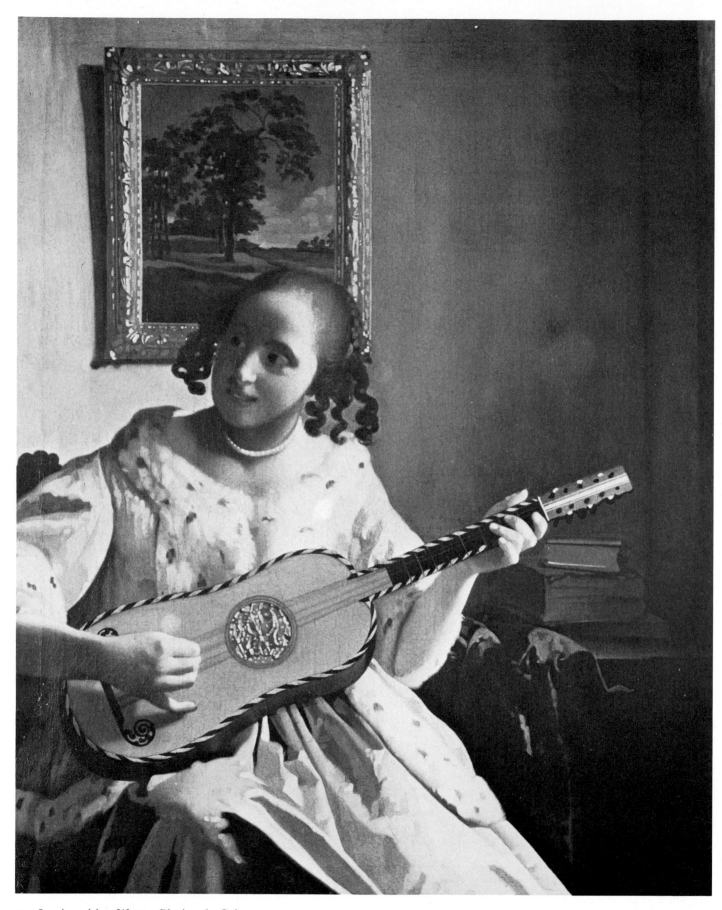

32 *Interior with a Woman Playing the Guitar*
LONDON, Kenwood House, The Iveagh Bequest. Canvas 53 × 46.3 cm. Signed half-way down on the right: IVMeer

Generally thought to have been the picture described as 'een personagie spelende op een cyter' which was ceded, along with the Beit *Interior* (Plate 30), by the artist's widow to a local baker in

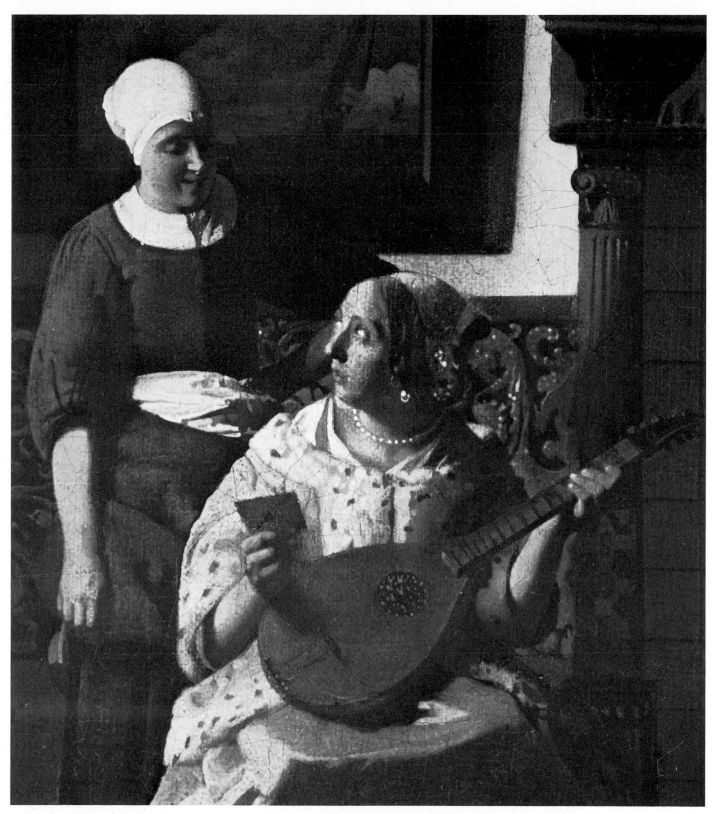

January 1676, it possibly was lot 4 in the 1696 sale. If this is so then Dissius, as a Vermeer collector, must have acquired it actually after the artist's death rather than as a direct commission to Vermeer himself. The history of the picture is then lost until it was brought to England in 1794 by the second viscount Palmerston, passing by descent until 1888. Agnew sold it in 1889 to the earl of Iveagh, who, in turn, bequeathed it in 1927, along with the rest of his collection, to the then London County Council. This is one of the few pictures by Vermeer which is known in a good old copy, in the Johnson Collection, Philadelphia. The history of the two pictures has often been confused, especially as the Johnson copy long enjoyed a reputation as the original. *The Guitar Player* is a rarity among seventeenth century pictures in general as it has never been relined.

(*above*)
Interior with a Lady Reading a Letter with her Maid (detail) Plate 29

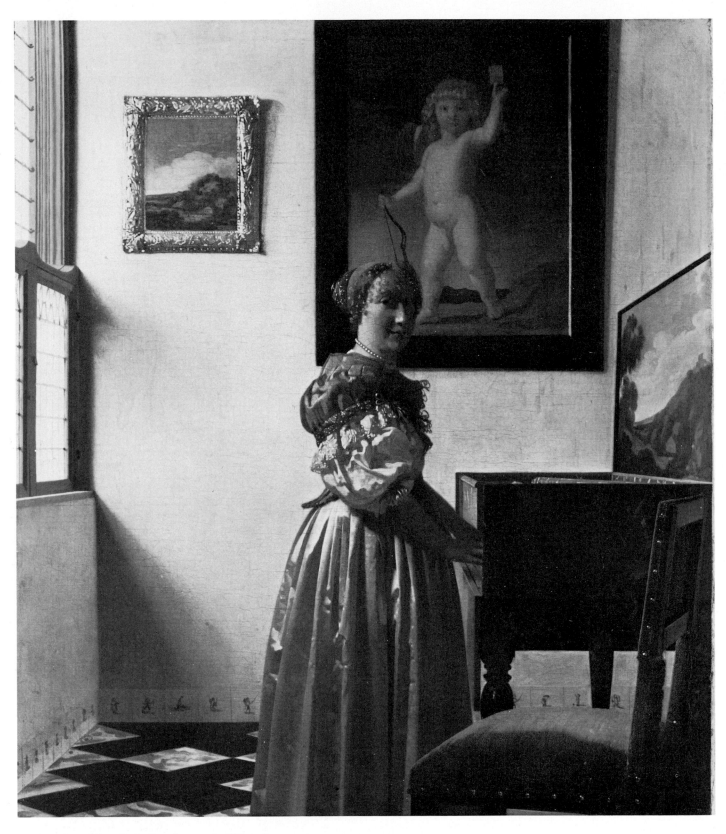

33 *Interior with a Lady Standing at the Virginals*
LONDON, National Gallery. Canvas 51.7 × 45.2 cm. Signed on the top left corner of the side of the virginals: IVMeer

Probably lot 37 in the 1696 sale, although this is by no means certain, the picture may have been in an anonymous sale, Amsterdam, 11 July 1714, but, again, this description could apply also to the *Lady Seated at the Virginals* (Plate 35). It appeared in an Amsterdam sale in 1797 and may have belonged to Edward Solly but this, too, is not certain. The *Lady Standing at the Virginals* made only 15 guineas when sold in the Edward William Lake sale, London, 12 July 1845, and was sold again in London in 1855, passing by 1866 into the collection of Thoré-Bürger himself. Sold with the rest of Thoré-Bürger's collection in Paris in 1892, it was acquired by Messrs. Lawrie of London for 29,000 francs, from whom it was purchased by the National Gallery in the same month.

Interior with a Lady Standing at the Virginals (detail)

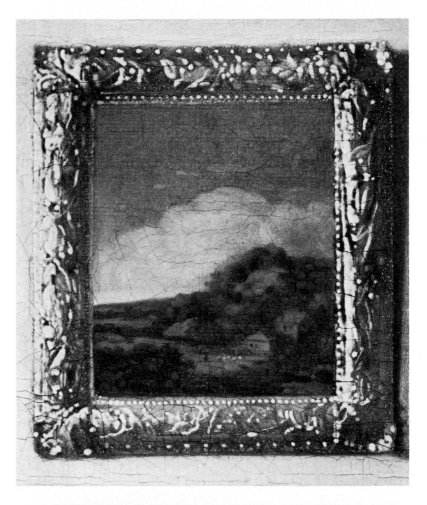

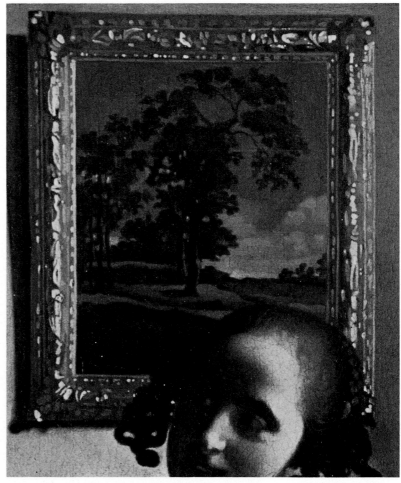

Interior with a Woman Playing the Guitar (detail)
Plate 32

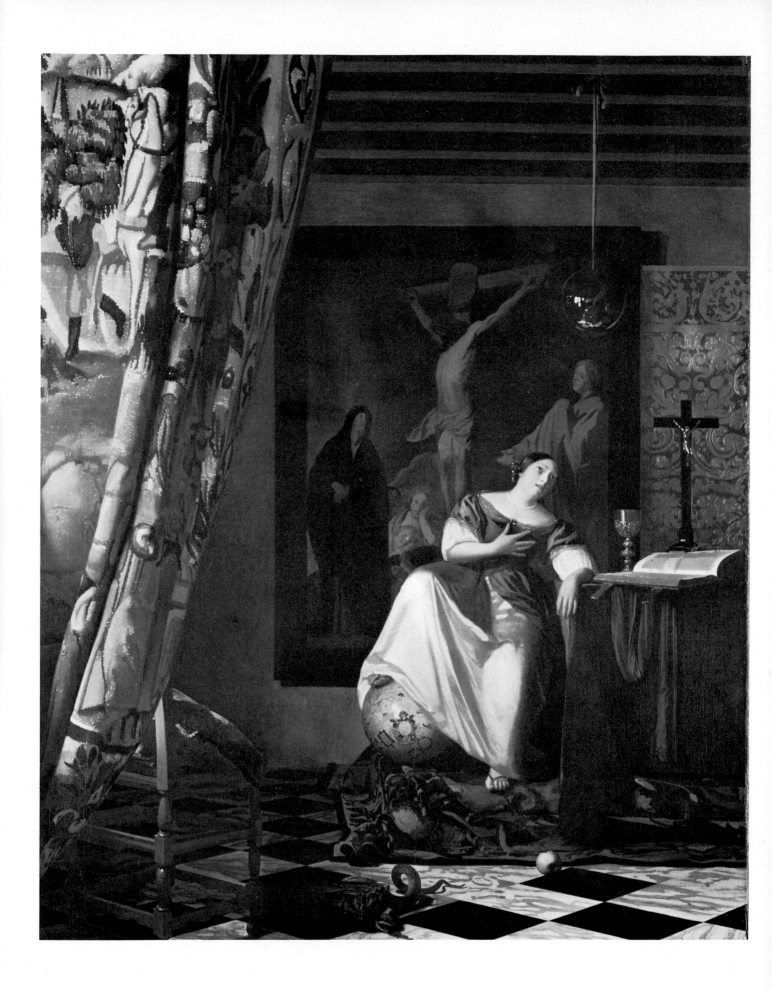

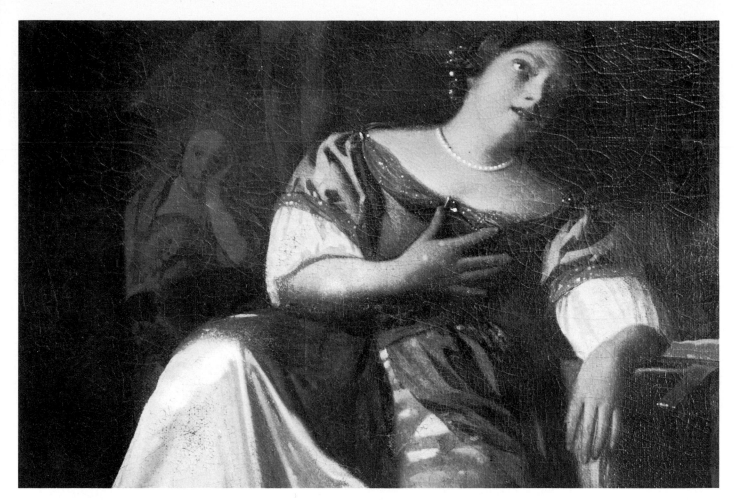

An Allegory of Faith (detail)

34 *An Allegory of Faith*
NEW YORK, Metropolitan Museum of Art. Canvas 113 × 89 cm. Unsigned

Described as an 'Allegory of the New Testament' in 1699, when it appeared in the Amsterdam sale of Herman van Swoll, making, for a painting by Vermeer, the high price of 400 florins, it was sold again in 1718, the price having risen to 500 florins. In 1735, however, its market value had fallen to 53 florins. It was sold again in Amsterdam in 1749. For the next 75 years *An Allegory of Faith* was in limbo until it appeared in the Oostenwijk collection in 1824, passing into the Stchoukine collection, Moscow, with the not entirely ridiculous attribution to Eglon van der Neer, even though the picture, at the same time, bore the false signature of Caspar Netscher. Sold by the dealer Wachtler, Berlin, to the distinguished Rembrandt scholar Abraham Bredius for 700 marks, again as a work of van der Neer, *An Allegory of Faith* was first attributed to Vermeer by Max J. Friedländer. Bredius lent the picture to the Mauritshuis, The Hague, of which institution he was director, and, later, it was in the hands of F. Kleinberger, Paris, who sold it to Colonel M. Friedsam, New York, who, in turn, bequeathed it to the Metropolitan Museum in 1931. This picture obviously annoyed Hofstede de Groot, who described Vermeer's few allegories as empty and tiresome.

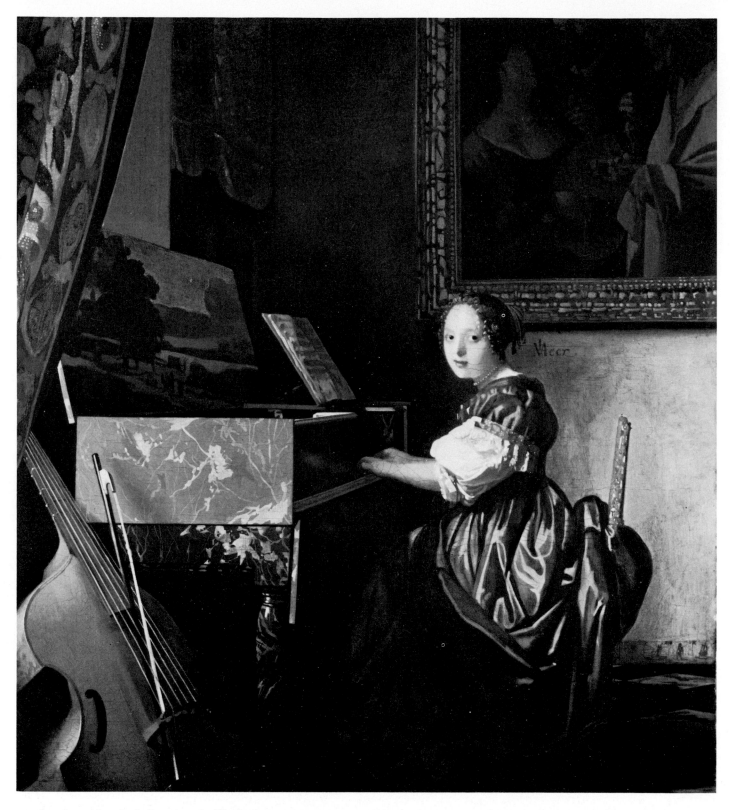

35 *Interior with a Lady Seated at the Virginals*
LONDON, National Gallery. Canvas 51.5 × 45.5 cm. Signed on the wall to the right of the head of the woman: IMeer

The descriptions from the 1696 sale and another sale of 1714 could well refer to the National Gallery *Lady Standing at the Virginals* (Plate 33), rather than to this one. The *Lady Seated at the Virginals* certainly was in the celebrated picture gallery of the graf von Schönborn at Pommersfelden near Bamberg and was acquired by Thoré-Bürger in 1867 at a Paris sale. Sold with the rest of the latter's collection in 1892, it was purchased by Sedelmeyer, who sold it to Messrs. Lawrie of London. The *Lady Seated* was then owned by T. Humphrey Ward and, by 1900, was in the collection of George Salting, who bequeathed it, along with the rest of his extensive collection, to the National Gallery in 1910. Thus, the *Lady Standing* and the *Lady Seated* were together in Thoré-Bürger's collection and were brought back together in the National Gallery in 1910, an accidental juxtaposition that often has led people into thinking, quite wrongly, that the pictures are pendants.

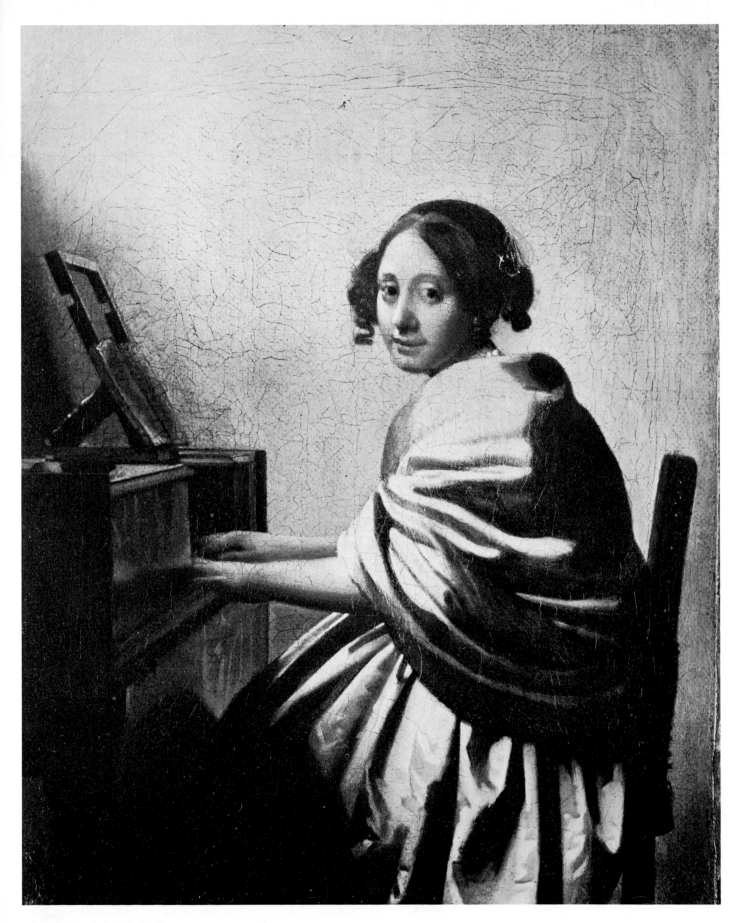

36 *A Lady at the Virginals*
Collection of Baron Rolin. Canvas 23.5 × 18.5 cm. Unsigned
Appearing in the Reyers sale, Amsterdam, 1814, the picture was in Sir Alfred Beit's collection in 1908, when Hofstede de Groot considered it authentic. It came to be rejected by most critics, but as it is now inaccessible there is a tendency to restore it to the artist's oeuvre; Gowing and Goldscheider accepted it.

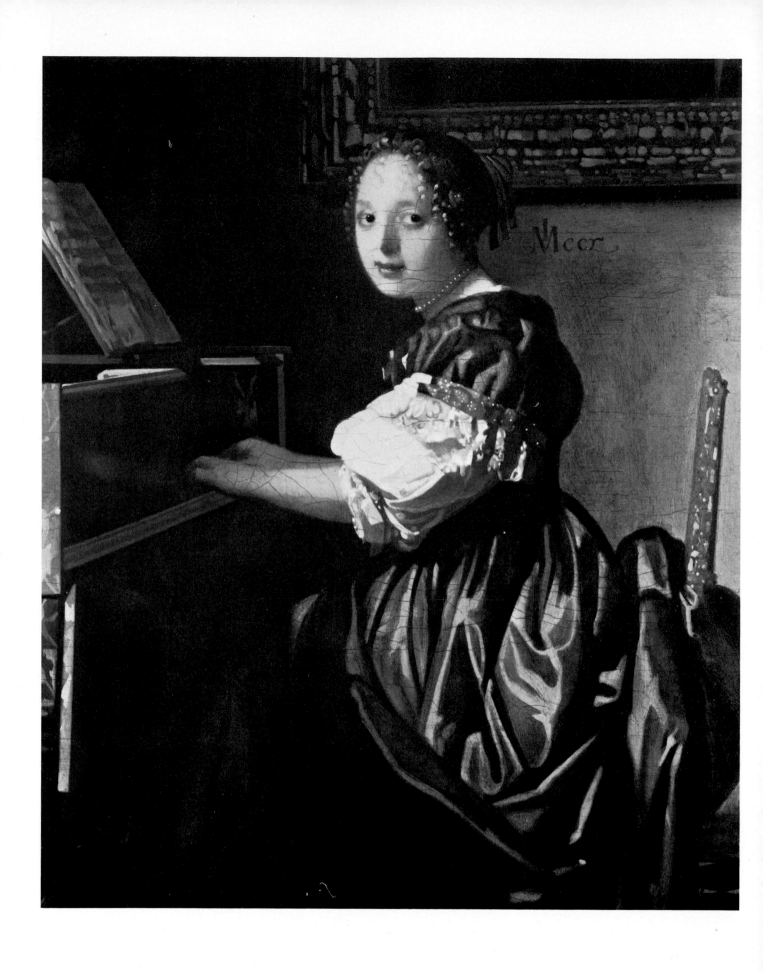

Interior with a Lady Seated at the Virginals (detail) Plate 35

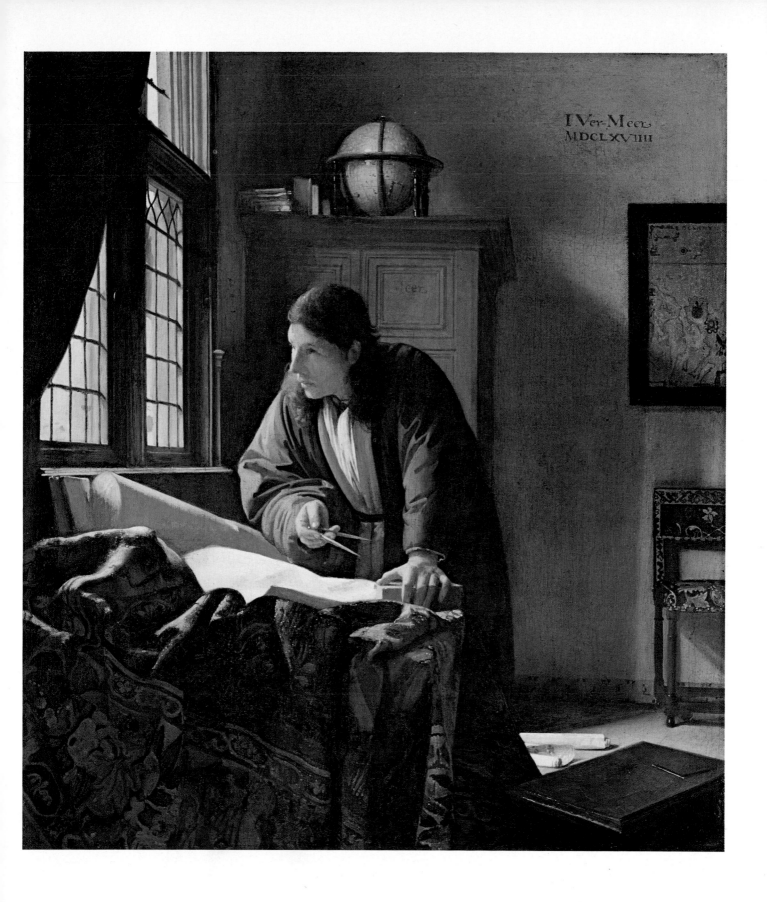

VII *Interior with a Geographer* (Plate 27)
Frankfurt–am–Main, Städelsches Kunstinstitut

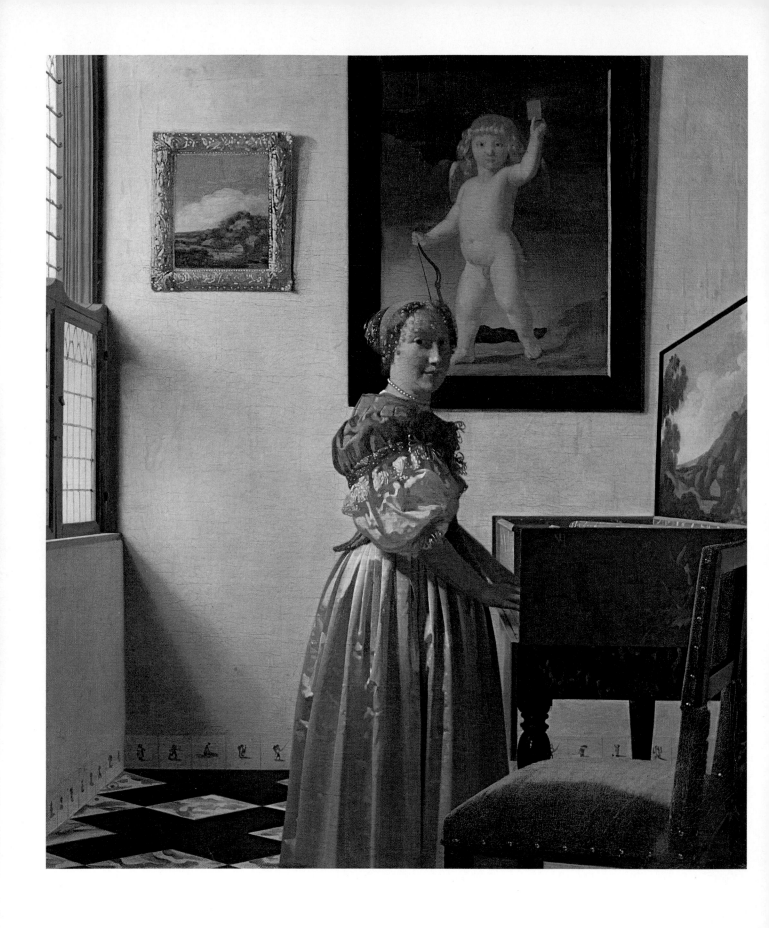

VIII *Interior with a Lady Standing at the Virginals* (Plate 33)
London, National Gallery

Biography

1632   Vermeer was born in the town of Delft and was baptised Johannes Reyniersoon Vermeer in the Nieuwe Kerk on 31 October. No record survives of his youth and education.

1653   Vermeer married Catherine Bolenes (or Bolnes) on 5 April. She was to bear him eleven children, eight of whom were still minors at the time of the artist's death in 1675. On 29 December Vermeer was received into the Guild of St. Luke at Delft but was able to make only part of the payment necessary for entry.

1654   The artist probably painted the *Esther before Ahasuerus* (fig. 2), his first surviving picture.

1655   Vermeer probably painted the *St. Praxedis* (fig. 3).

1656   The year of the Dresden *Procuress* (Plate 3). This is the last picture to bear a date until 1668.

1662   Vermeer became a *hoofdman*, literally 'head man', of the Guild, which would indicate a rise in his status.

1663   Monsieur Balthasar de Montconys visited Delft, where he complained that he was not able to see any pictures by Vermeer in his studio. Only one picture was visible at all and that was in the hands of a local baker, who, in Montconys's opinion, had paid too much for it considering that the subject was limited to a single figure. This remark was made in his *Journal de Voyage* (Lyons, 1666). Vermeer again became a *hoofdman* of the Guild.

1667   Vermeer was briefly mentioned in a couplet by D. van Bleyswyck in his *Beschryvinge der Stadt Delft*.

1668   The artist dated his painting of *The Astronomer* (Plate 26).

1669   Vermeer probably painted the Frankfurt *Geographer* (Plate 27) as a pendant to *The Astronomer*.

1670   The artist was again recorded as a *hoofdman* of the Guild and also in the following year.

1672   Vermeer was described in a document as an expert in Italian paintings which is evidence of his activity as an art dealer.

1675   Vermeer died in poverty. He left many debts and only a few pictures and was buried in the Oude Kerk at Delft on 15 December.

fig. 7 Johannes MEYSSENS, after Vermeer
Self-portrait of Vermeer
Engraving   dimensions unknown

This engraving is inscribed 'Ver Meer pinxit'.
It forms a plausible record of a now lost
painting of the young artist in his studio,
and it would be reasonable to assume that
Vermeer was not much more than thirty
years of age when this picture was painted.
There is, in the collection of John and Joanna
Bass, Miami Beach, Florida, a painting which
has been claimed as the original by Vermeer
on which this engraving was based.

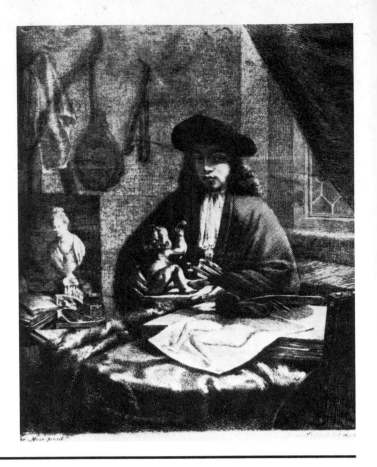

A History of Vermeer's Pictures and his Reputation

THE FOLLOWING SERIES of disjointed facts sets out to record in chronological order the different occasions when Vermeer's pictures have been bought and sold and to analyse the pattern which emerges. The first fifty years after the artist's death saw considerable activity in the buying and selling of his pictures as a commodity for collectors, but the artist's name then disappeared into oblivion, only to be revived by Thoré-Bürger as late as 1866.

1676	24 January: a picture which could well have been the Vienna *Artist's Studio* (Plate 28) appeared as security for a loan made by Vermeer's mother-in-law to his widow.
	27 January: two pictures were ceded by the artist's widow to a baker in payment for an outstanding bill. Their descriptions were very vague, but the pictures are usually identified with the Beit *Interior with a Lady Writing a Letter* (Plate 30) and the Kenwood *Guitar Player* (Plate 32).
1696	16 May: an anonymous sale was held in Amsterdam containing over one hundred pictures, twenty-one of which were described as by Vermeer of Delft. Modern research has shown that the seller probably was Jacob Abrahamsz. Dissius, a bookseller of Delft. This is the most important source for the early identification of Vermeer's pictures, but the descriptions given in the sale catalogue itself are often ambiguous. An approximate translation is given here together with the possible present identifications and locations of the pictures.

1. 'A young woman weighing gold in a small case by J. van der Meer of Delft 155 florins'. This is usually identified with the Washington *Woman Weighing Gold* (Plate 25).

2. 'A maid pouring out milk especially good by the same 175 florins'. This has always been identified with the Amsterdam *Maidservant Pouring Milk* (Plate 7).

3. 'Portrait of Vermeer with various accessories in a room uncommonly well painted 45 florins'. This entry has been associated with the Vienna *Artist's Studio*, but, in fact, this is unlikely, because it would be unusual for so large a picture to be valued at as little as 45 florins.

4. 'A young woman playing a guitar very good by the same 70 florins'. This is usually identified with the Kenwood *Guitar Player*. If this is so then Dissius must have acquired it from the baker (see above '1676').

5. 'A gentleman washing his hands in a room with a through view with pictures artistic and unusual by the same 95 florins'. No picture corresponding to this subject has ever been attributed to Vermeer, and, at present, it must be considered lost.

6. 'A young woman playing a virginal in a room with a man listening to her 80 florins'. This description more or less corresponds to the Windsor *Music Lesson* (Plate 14).

7. 'A young woman with her maid with a letter 70 florins'. Both the Amsterdam *Interior with a Lady with her Maid* (Plate 29) and the Frick picture (Plate 17) of the same subject are possible candidates for identification with this entry.

8. 'A drunken sleeping maid at a table 62 florins'. This is likely to be the New York *Woman Asleep* (Plate 4).

9. 'A cheerful group of people in a room 73 florins'. Both the Brunswick *Interior* (Plate 12) and the Dresden *Procuress* (Plate 3) could be described as cheerful, but, of course, this lot is just as likely to be a further work by Vermeer which is now lost.

10. 'A music making man and a young woman in a room 81 florins'. This picture must be presumed lost as we do not have any picture by Vermeer with a *man* making music.

11. 'A soldier and a laughing girl very fine 44 florins'. This picture is reasonably identified with the Frick painting of the same subject (Plate 9).

12. 'A young woman making lace 28 florins'. This is likely to be the Louvre *Lacemaker* (Plate 31).

31. 'The town of Delft in perspective viewed from the South by J. van der Meer of Delft 200 florins'. The famous *View of Delft* (Plate 5) was valued higher than any other picture in the sale.

32. 'A view of a house in Delft 72 florins'. Reasonably identified with the Amsterdam *Little Street* (Plate 6), which, however, could equally well have been no. 33 below.

33. 'A view of another house, ditto, 48 florins'. Either this picture or the one above is now lost.

35. 'A young lady writing by the same very good 63 florins'. This is, presumably, the Washington *Lady Writing a Letter* (Plate 16).

36. 'A young woman adorning herself very fine 30 florins'. This is quite possibly the Berlin *Young Woman with a Pearl Necklace* (Plate 24).

37. 'A young lady playing the virginals 42 florins'. At least three surviving pictures could answer this description: the two in the National Gallery, London (Plates 33 and 35) and the little picture now in Baron Rolin's collection (Plate 36).

38. 'A portrait in antique costume uncommonly artistic 36 florins'. This is often associated with the Hague *Girl with a Pearl Earring* (Plate 19), although the picture in a New York private collection (Plate 18) also answers this description.

39 and 40. Ditto of no. 38, 17 florins each. These well could be the two tiny heads in Washington (Plates 20 and 21).

<table>
<tr><td>1699</td><td>22 April: the New York Allegory of Faith (Plate 34) was sold for 400 florins, a considerable price bearing in mind that in the Dissius sale, three years before, all twenty-one pictures were sold each for 200 florins or less.</td></tr>
</table>

FOR THE WHOLE of the eighteenth century Vermeer's name was forgotten but his pictures were appearing constantly in the saleroom. These ephemeral catalogues form the only printed records of the artist's reputation for more than a century.

1701	20 April: the Washington *Woman Weighing Gold* and the Amsterdam *Milkmaid* were sold together in Amsterdam for 113 and 320 florins respectively.
1710	The *Interior with Two Gentlemen and a Girl with a Wineglass* (Plate 12) was recorded in the collection of Anton Ulrich, Duke of Brunswick-Wolfenbüttel. He could have acquired the picture earlier.
1712	The Amsterdam *Lady Reading* (Plate 23) was sold in Amsterdam for 110 florins. This identification, however, is not definite.
1713	*The Geographer* (Plate 27) and *The Astronomer* (Plate 26) were sold together in Rotterdam for 300 florins.
1714	A picture described as a *Lady at the Virginals* was sold in Amsterdam for 55 florins. Both pictures in the National Gallery, London and the Windsor *Music Lesson* have been considered as possible candidates for identification with this vague description.
1718	The New York *Allegory of Faith* was sold in Amsterdam for the relatively high sum of 500 florins.
1719	The Amsterdam *Milkmaid* was sold in Amsterdam for 126 florins.
1720	After a gap of only seven years *The Geographer* and *The Astronomer* were sold together again, this time for the much reduced price of 160 florins.
1729	The price of *The Astronomer* and *The Geographer* fell still further. They were sold together again in Amsterdam for 106 florins.
1730	The Beit *Interior* (Plate 30) was sold in Rotterdam for 155 florins.
1735	The reappearance of the New York *Allegory of Faith* revealed a dramatic fall in its value; this time it made only 53 florins.
1736	The Berlin *Interior* (Plate 10) was sold in Delft for 52 florins.
1737	The New York *Woman Asleep* was sold in Amsterdam for a little more than 8 florins. This was the lowest price so far for a painting by Vermeer.
1738	The Frick *Lady with her Maid* (Plate 17) was sold for 160 florins in Amsterdam.
1741	Augustus III, Elector of Saxony, acquired *The Procuress* (Plate 3) for his picture gallery at Dresden.
1742	Augustus III added the *Girl at a Window* (Plate 8) to his collection.
1749	The New York *Allegory of Faith* reappeared at auction in Amsterdam. This time it fared a little better and made 70 florins.
1762	King George III of England acquired the Windsor *Music Lesson* as a work by Frans van Mieris.
1765	The Amsterdam *Milkmaid* was auctioned in Amsterdam for 560 florins.
1768	*The Milkmaid* reappeared at auction, and the price rose to 925 florins.
1769	The Washington *Woman Weighing Gold* made 170 florins at auction in Amsterdam.
1772	The Amsterdam *Lady Reading* was sold in Amsterdam for an unknown price.
1777	The resale of the *Woman Weighing Gold* in Amsterdam caused the price to rise to 235 florins.
1778	For the first time since the 1696 sale a group of pictures by Vermeer were sold together. It consisted of *The Astronomer* and *The Geographer*, which together made 172 florins, and the Louvre *Lacemaker*, which must have been much more esteemed as it made 150 florins alone.
1780	The Boston *Concert* (Plate 15) was auctioned in Amsterdam for 315 florins.

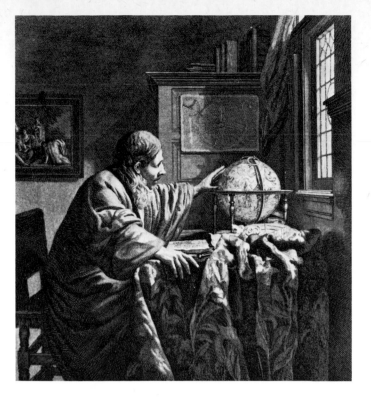

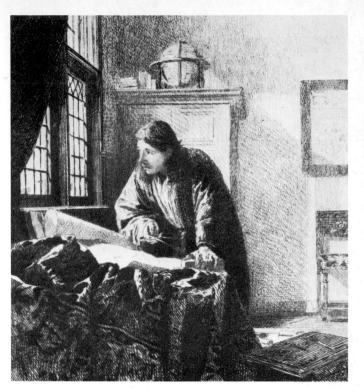

fig. 8 Louis GARREAU, after Vermeer
The Astronomer
Engraving 19.4 × 16.5 cm.

This engraving is dated 1784, when *The Astronomer* belonged to Le Brun, the art dealer and collector husband of the painter Elisabeth Vigée-Le Brun. The engraving shows that much more was visible in the picture than can be seen today. This is particularly obvious in the picture hanging on the wall.

fig. 9 Charles-Théodore DEBLOIS, after Vermeer
The Geographer
Engraving 10 × 9 cm.

An inferior engraving made when *The Geographer* was on the Vienna art market in 1885. The execution is so summary that it does not even record the appearance of the two signatures on the picture.

THE DISTURBANCES of the French Revolution and the Napoleonic era brought an enormous number of works of art on to the market, especially those from aristocratic collections which had been more or less static for a generation or two. The uncertain political situation could well have contributed to the fluctuation in prices.

1791	The Amsterdam *Lady Reading* was sold for 43 florins.
1793	The picture reappeared in the saleroom and, this time, made 70 florins.
1797	Another small group of pictures by Vermeer was sold, *The Astronomer* and *The Geographer*, which together made 133 florins, accompanied by the London *Lady Standing at the Virginals*, which made either 19 or 49 florins.
1798	The Amsterdam *Milkmaid* was sold for 1550 florins, an amazing price considering Vermeer's lack of fashion at the time.
1800	Another high price, 1040 florins, was paid for a picture by Vermeer, this time for *The Little Street*. In another sale in the same year, however, *The Astronomer*, now separated from *The Geographer*, made only 270 florins. *The Astronomer* had belonged to the art dealer Le Brun.
1801	The Amsterdam *Lady Reading* reappeared on the market after only a decade. This time it made 110 florins.
1802	The Frick *Lady with her Maid* was sold in Paris for 2000 francs.
1804	The Boston *Concert* made only 350 florins in a Paris sale.

1809	The Amsterdam *Lady Reading* appeared yet again. It was sold in Paris for 200 francs, while the Berlin *Woman with a Pearl Necklace* made only 55 florins in Amsterdam.
1810	The Louvre *Lacemaker* was sold in Rotterdam, and the Frick *Girl Interrupted at her Music* was sold in Amsterdam for 610 florins, while the Frick *Lady with her Maid* was sold in Paris for 601 francs.
1811	Three pictures which recently had been sold all reappeared at auction, the Louvre *Lacemaker*, the Frick *Girl Interrupted at her Music* (399 florins) and the Berlin *Woman with a Pearl Necklace* (36 florins).
1813	In the Muilman sale in Amsterdam the Louvre *Lacemaker* made 84 florins, while the Amsterdam *Milkmaid* held its price at 2125 florins. The Vienna *Artist's Studio* entered the collection of the grafen von Czernin as a work by Pieter de Hoogh.
1814	The Rolin *Lady at the Virginals* (Plate 36) was sold in Amsterdam for 30 florins.
1815	The Louvre *Lacemaker* fell to 19 florins in an anonymous sale in Amsterdam.

THE RETURN OF peace to northern Europe in 1815 did little to alter the pattern of constant sale and resale of Vermeer's pictures, and it was not until c. 1830 that trade seemed to fall off. There followed a quiet period when the lowest prices seem to have been on the English art market, a nadir which was reached just before Thoré-Bürger's dramatic rehabilitation of the artist in 1866.

1816	In Rotterdam, in an anonymous sale, two small heads were sold for very little, while the Washington *Lady Writing a Letter* made 70 florins. It was described as by Vermeer.
1817	The Louvre *Lacemaker* appeared in a Paris sale.
1818	The Frick *Lady with her Maid* was sold in Paris for 46 francs.
1820	The Frick *Girl Interrupted at her Music* was bought at auction by Brondgeest for 340 florins.
1822	*The View of Delft* was sold in Amsterdam for 2900 florins. It was acquired immediately by the Dutch government and placed in the Royal Cabinet of Pictures at The Hague. The Washington *Girl in a Red Hat* was sold in Paris for 200 francs.
1825	The Washington *Lady Writing a Letter* was sold in Rotterdam for 305 florins, and the Amsterdam *Lady Reading* was sold in Paris for 2060 francs.
1826	The Washington *Woman Weighing Gold* was sold for 800 florins as having come from the collection of Maximilian I Joseph, King of Bavaria.
1827	The Washington *Lady Writing a Letter* reappeared in an Amsterdam saleroom.
1830	The Washington *Woman Weighing Gold* was sold in Paris for 2410 francs.
1833	*The Geographer* was sold in Amsterdam for 195 florins.
1837	The Washington *Woman Weighing Gold* appeared yet again in the saleroom; this time it made 400 francs. The Frick *Lady with her Maid* was sold from the cabinet of the noted collector the duchesse de Berri for 415 francs.
1845	The London *Lady Standing at the Virginals* was in the Edward William Lake sale at Christie's.
1848	The Washington *Woman Weighing Gold* was sold at the Casimir Perier sale, Christie's, for £141 and 15 shillings.
1851	The Louvre *Lacemaker* was sold in The Hague for 260 florins.
1853	The Frick *Girl Interrupted at her Music* appeared at Christie's in the Samuel Woodburn sale and was sold for £42.
1854	Van der Hoop bequeathed the *Lady Reading* to the city of Amsterdam.
1855	The National Gallery *Lady Standing at the Virginals* was sold in London for 14½ guineas.
1856	The Berlin *Woman with a Pearl Necklace* was sold in Amsterdam for 111 florins.

1860	The Boston *Concert* was sold at Christie's, London, for £21.

1866   Perhaps the most important moment in the whole history of Vermeer's pictures, Thoré-Bürger published his two-part article in the *Gazette des Beaux-Arts* which assembled a surprisingly high proportion of the pictures and also the biographical facts which are known today. Thoré-Bürger, the pseudonym of Etienne-Joseph Théophile Thoré (1807–1869), was an avid collector of the originals, owning several including the Berlin *Woman with a Pearl Necklace*, and his work was based largely on original research as there was no accumulation of printed sources on which he could rely. From this time onwards dealers and connoisseurs had a point of reference on which they could rely and from which they could profit.

1867   Thoré-Bürger acquired the National Gallery *Lady Seated at the Virginals* for 2000 francs.

1868   The Berlin *Woman with a Pearl Necklace* was sold in Brussels for 3500 francs. It must have been acquired by Thoré-Bürger soon afterwards.

1870   The Louvre *Lacemaker* was sold in Paris and was subsequently acquired by the Louvre for 7500 francs.

1874   The then Kaiser Friedrich Museum in Berlin acquired the *Woman with a Pearl Necklace* with the rest of the Suermondt collection.

1876   The Hague *Diana* (Plate 2) was sold in Paris for 10,000 francs, as by Nicolas Maes. It was acquired by the Mauritshuis soon after.

1877   The New York *Girl with a Jug* (Plate 13) was sold at Christie's for £404 and 5 shillings.

1880   In the Demidov sale, San Donato, Florence, the Frankfurt *Geographer* was sold for 22,000 lire.

1881   The Beit *Interior* was sold to E. Secrétan in Paris for 60,000 francs, and the Frick *Soldier with a Girl Laughing* was sold for 88,000 francs in the Léopold Double sale, along with *The Astronomer*, which made 44,000 francs.

1882   A. A. des Tombe acquired The Hague *Head of a Girl* for two and one-half florins.

1885   The Städelsches Kunstinstitut at Frankfurt acquired *The Geographer*.

1888   Henry G. Marquand gave the *Girl with a Jug* to the Metropolitan Museum, New York.

1889   The Frick *Lady with her Maid* and the Beit *Interior* appeared together in the E. Secrétan sale in Paris and made 75,000 francs and 62,000 francs respectively.

1892   The Thoré-Bürger sale marked another turning point in the history of Vermeer's pictures. Never again was a group such as this to be sold at auction. Quite a number of Vermeer's pictures were already in the great galleries of Europe, in Paris, Berlin, Dresden, Brunswick, Frankfurt, Amsterdam and The Hague. The rest were to become the property of the very rich and subsequently found their way into the museums of England and the eastern seaboard of America. The Thoré-Bürger sale took place on 5 December. The *Lady Standing at the Virginals* was bought by Messrs. Lawrie of London for 29,000 francs, the *Lady Seated at the Virginals* was bought by Sedelmeyer for 25,000 francs and *The Concert* was bought by Robert for 29,000 francs for Mrs. Gardner. The National Gallery acquired the *Lady Standing at the Virginals* from Messrs. Lawrie.

1893   The Rijksmuseum bought the *Interior with a Lady Reading a Letter with her Maid*.

1897   Collis P. Huntington bequeathed the *Interior with a Woman Playing the Lute* (Plate 22) to the Metropolitan Museum, New York.

1901   Henry Clay Frick acquired the *Interior with a Girl Interrupted at her Music*, and Wilhelm von Bode bought the *Interior with a Gentleman and a Young Woman with a Wineglass* for the Kaiser Friedrich Museum, Berlin.

1903   A. A. des Tombe bequeathed the *Head of a Girl* to the Mauritshuis, The Hague.

1907   The Rijksmuseum, Amsterdam, acquired the *Maidservant Pouring Milk*.

1910   George Salting bequeathed the *Lady Seated at the Virginals* to the National Gallery, London.

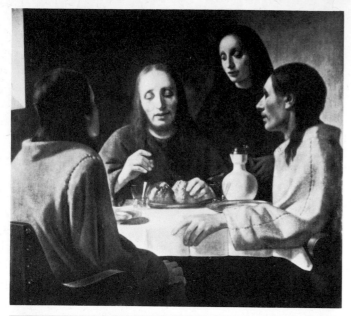

fig. 10 Hans van MEEGEREN, forgery of Vermeer
The Supper at Emmaus
Canvas 117 × 129 cm.
Rotterdam, Boymans van Beuningen Museum

Van Meegeren's most successful forgery of Vermeer, the picture was discovered and published by Dr. Bredius in *The Burlington Magazine* in 1937. Bredius wrote 'It is a wonderful moment in the life of a lover of Vermeer when he finds himself suddenly confronted with a hitherto unknown painting by a great master, untouched, on the original canvas, and without any restoration, just as it left the painter's studio'. Following the exposure of van Meegeren after the war the picture was not without its defenders. Jean Decoen wrote a carefully argued book, *Vermeer-van Meegeren, Back to the Truth* (Rotterdam, 1951), in which he rightly assumed that *The Supper at Emmaus* was very much better than van Meegeren's other forgeries but wrongly concluded that it was by Vermeer himself.

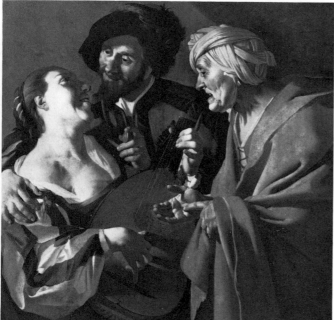

fig. 11 Dirck van BABUREN
The Procuress
Canvas 101 × 107.5 cm.
Signed
Boston, Museum of Fine Arts (Purchased, Maria T. B. Hopkins Fund)

This picture came to light at a London auction in 1949 and was acquired later by the Boston Museum. It is a good example of the type of Caravaggesque art practised by all three Utrecht masters, Baburen, Terbrugghen and Honthorst. Another copy is in the Rijksmuseum, Amsterdam. *The Procuress* appears in the background of two paintings by Vermeer (Plates 15 and 35).

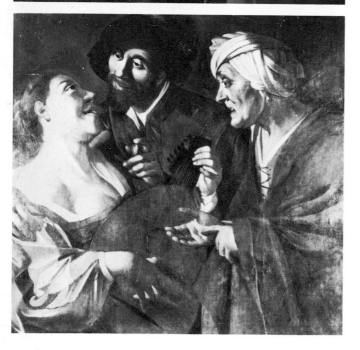

fig. 12 Hans van MEEGEREN, forgery of Baburen
The Procuress
Canvas 76 × 96.5 cm.
London, Courtauld Institute of Art

In comparison with the original painting by Baburen (fig. 11), this picture looks like a weak caricature, yet van Meegeren's deception was successful at the time.

1911	Henry Clay Frick acquired the *Interior with a Soldier and a Girl Laughing*.
1913	Benjamin Altman bequeathed the *Interior with a Woman Asleep* to the Metropolitan Museum, New York.
1919	Henry Clay Frick bought the *Lady with her Maid* from Duveen.
1921	*The Little Street* was given to the Rijksmuseum by Sir Henry Deterding.
1927	The *Christ in the House of Martha and Mary* was given to the National Gallery of Scotland in memory of W. A. Coats, and the earl of Iveagh bequeathed the *Lady Playing the Guitar* to the London County Council.
1931	Colonel M. Friedsam bequeathed the *Allegory of Faith* to the Metropolitan Museum, New York.
1937	Apart from Andrew Mellon's gift of the *Girl in a Red Hat* to the National Gallery, Washington, an otherwise black year in the history of Vermeer's reputation. An astonishing picture was published by none other than Dr. Bredius. Entitled *The Supper at Emmaus* (fig. 10) and acquired for an enormous sum by the Boymans Museum at Rotterdam, it seemed to give a new dimension to Vermeer's early work. Several other pictures, obviously related, appeared at this time. The only convincing explanation for the almost universal acceptance of *The Supper at Emmaus* as a masterpiece is the importance of the scholar responsible for its publication.
c. 1939	Adolf Hitler removed the Czernin *Artist's Studio* from the Czernin family collection and took it to Berchtesgarten.
1942	Joseph Widener gave the *Girl with a Flute* and the *Woman Weighing Gold* to the National Gallery, Washington.
1946	The Czernin *Artist's Studio* was acquired by the Vienna gallery after the picture was discovered hidden safely in a salt mine. A Dutch painter called Hans van Meegeren was accused by the restored Dutch government of having sold pictures by Vermeer to Goering during the war. In order to defend himself he claimed to have painted them himself, including *The Supper at Emmaus*. Van Meegeren was able to prove himself the author of the whole group of pictures by painting a similar work in prison. To modern eyes van Meegeren's pictures belong to the world of the 1930s cinema screen epitomised by Greta Garbo and, in spite of their childishness from a stylistic point of view, van Meegeren's work caught popular imagination as an example of how all the experts of the time were so easily deceived. What is never said is how willing the public is to accept the words of the experts without looking at the pictures they are promoting.
1955	Mr. and Mrs. Charles B. Wrightsman acquired the *Portrait of a Young Woman*, formerly in the Arenberg collection.
1962	The National Gallery in Washington was given the *Interior with a Lady Writing a Letter* in memory of Horace Havemeyer.

THE LAST FEW years have seen the rise of a new trend, that of using famous works of art for political reasons, either for ransom or in order to bring attention to a specific cause. Significantly, the people responsible have always chosen great works of art to further their ends, and Vermeer's pictures rank high on this list. Within three years almost 10% of his surviving output has suffered theft and damage.

1971	While on exhibition in Brussels the Amsterdam *Lady Reading a Letter with her Maid* was stolen and, in the process, damaged quite seriously, especially round the edges.
1974	The Kenwood *Guitar Player* was stolen for political reasons but was returned undamaged, although its destruction had been threatened. The Beit *Interior* also was stolen, along with many other pictures from the collection, but was subsequently found with only slight damage.

Bibliography and Concordance

THE VERY FIRST study of Vermeer appeared as a two part article entitled 'Van der Meer de Delft' in the French periodical *Gazette des Beaux-Arts* in 1866. Its author was Thoré-Bürger. Some of the attributions to Vermeer which he included are no longer accepted today, but the article remains a model of detective work based on a thorough knowledge of the collections of Europe. This was followed in 1908 by Cornelis Hofstede de Groot's monumental *Catalogue Raisonné of the Works of the Most Eminent Dutch Painters of the 17th Century*, vol. IX, pp. 587–607, in which he amplified and brought up to date Thoré-Bürger's work.

There were several short and well-written critical studies in the early twentieth century, in particular that

		1696 Sale	Thoré (1866)	HdG (190
1	*Christ in the House of Martha and Mary* (Edinburgh)	—	—	1
2	*Diana and her Companions* (The Hague)	—	—	3
3	*The Procuress* (Dresden)	lot 9 (?)	1	41
4	*Interior with a Woman Asleep* (New York)	lot 8	—	16
5	*The View of Delft* (The Hague)	lot 31	48	48
6	*The Little Street* (Amsterdam)	lot 32	49	47
7	*The Milkmaid* (Amsterdam)	lot 2	25	17
8	*Interior with a Girl at a Window Reading a Letter* (Dresden)	—	31	34
9	*Interior with a Soldier and a Girl Laughing* (New York)	lot 11	7	39
10	*Interior with a Gentleman and a Young Woman* (Berlin)	—	20	37
11	*Interior with a Girl Interrupted at her Music* (New York)	—	9	27
12	*Interior with Two Gentlemen and a Girl* (Brunswick)	lot 9 (?)	6	38
13	*Interior with a Girl at a Window with a Jug* (New York)	—	—	19
14	*The Music Lesson* (Windsor)	lot 6	10	28
15	*The Concert* (Boston)	—	23	29
16	*Interior with a Lady Writing a Letter* (Washington)	lot 35	40	36
17	*A Lady with her Maid* (New York)	lot 7 (?)	8	33
18	*A Young Woman* (New York)	lot 38 (?)	2	42

in French of Gustave Vanzype in 1908 (second edition, 1925), while the first serious modern catalogue was that in Dutch by A. B. de Vries in 1939 with his *Jan Vermeer van Delft*. The English edition of this book appeared in 1948 with van Meegeren's *Supper at Emmaus* removed. In 1952 the appearance of Lawrence Gowing's *Vermeer* meant that an important step forward had been made in the consideration of Vermeer's pictorial sources, and, although the book is difficult to read, it contains many observations of importance. After Gowing, two excellent anthologies appeared, that of Vitale Bloch in 1954, *Tutta la Pittura di Vermeer di Delft*, and that of Ludwig Goldscheider, with an introduction by Thomas

Bodkin, in 1958. The second edition of the latter came in 1967, and the reproductions are especially good.

The study of Vermeer by Giuseppe Ungaretti and Piero Bianconi, which appeared as part of the *Opera Completa* series in 1967, contains a useful anthology of the pictures wrongly attributed to Vermeer, including the work of van Meegeren. The most recent scholarly study is that of Albert Blankert with extensive documentation and catalogue by Rob Ruurs and Willem L. van de Watering. Blankert's book, *Johannes Vermeer* (1975), is the most thorough to date from a documentary point of view, but he has rejected too many of Vermeer's best pictures to be taken seriously as a critic.

Vries (1948)	Gowing (1952)	Bloch (1954)	Goldscheider (1958, 2nd ed. 1967)	Opera Completa (1967)	Blankert (1975)
2	1 (pls. 1–3)	2 (pls. 2–4)	1	3	1
1	4 (pls. 8–9)	1 (pl. 1)	2	1	2
3	2 (pls. 4–5)	3 (pls. 5–8)	4	5	3
4	3 (pls. 6–7)	4 (pls. 9–11)	3	7	4
8	13 (pls. 30–32)	8 (pls. 18–21)	10	11	10
7	7 (pls. 14–15)	16 (pls. 40–45)	7	10	9
9	8 (pls. 16–17)	7 (pls. 16–17)	9	12	7
5	5 (pls. 10–11)	5 (pls. 12–13)	6	8	6
6	6 (pls. 12–13)	6 (pls. 14–15)	5	9	5
11	9 (pls. 18–20)	9 (pls. 22–23)	11	14	8
13	10 (pl. 21)	10 (pls. 24–25)	12	18	B2
12	14 (pls. 33–36)	11 (pl. 26)	15	15	11
10	15 (pls. 38–39)	14 (pls. 35–37)	16	13	12
A	12 (pls. 24–29, 37)	12 (pls. 27–32)	13	20	16
14	11 (pls. 22–23)	13 (pls. 33–34)	14	19	17
19	18 (pl. 42)	22 (pl. 53)	20	28	20
25	25 (pls. 54–55)	32 (pls. 77–78)	29	33	21
15	17 (pl. 41)	17 (pl. 46)	34	23	30

	1696 Sale	Thoré (1866)	HdG (19
19 *Head of a Girl* (The Hague)	lot 38 (?)	—	44
20 *The Girl in a Red Hat* (Washington)	lots 39/40 ?	47	46A
21 *The Girl with a Flute* (Washington)	lots 39/40 (?)	—	22d
22 *Interior with a Woman Playing the Lute* (New York)	—	—	—
23 *Interior with a Lady Reading a Letter* (Amsterdam)	—	32	31
24 *Interior with a Woman with a Pearl Necklace* (Berlin)	lot 36	33	20
25 *Interior with a Woman Weighing Gold* (Washington)	lot 1	26/27	10
26 *The Astronomer* (Paris)	—	36	6
27 *The Geographer* (Frankfurt)	—	34	5
28 *The Artist's Studio* (Vienna)	lot 3 (?)	5	8
29 *Interior with a Lady Reading a Letter with her Maid* (Amsterdam)	lot 7 (?)	—	32
30 *Interior with a Lady Writing a Letter* (Blessington)	—	—	35
31 *The Lacemaker* (Paris)	lot 12	37	11
32 *The Guitar Player* (London)	lot 4 (?)	—	26
33 *Interior with a Lady Standing at the Virginals* (London)	lot 37 (?)	29	23
34 *An Allegory of Faith* (New York)	—	41	2
35 *Interior with a Lady Seated at the Virginals* (London)	lot 37 (?)	30	25
36 *A Lady at the Virginals* (Rolin collection)	lot 37 (?)	—	24

Vries (1948)	Gowing (1952)	Bloch (1954)	Goldscheider (1958, 2nd ed. 1967)	Opera Completa (1967)	Blankert (1975)
B	22 (pl. 49)	19 (pl. 49)	23	21	18
22	27 (pl. 57)	24 (pl. 56)	25	32	B3
?	26 (pl. 56)	25 (pl. 57)	26	31	B4
20	16 (pl. 40)	21 (pl. 52)	19	27	B1
C	21 (pls. 47–48)	18 (pls. 47–48)	17	26	14
18	19 (pl. 43)	20 (pls. 50–51)	18	25	13
17	20 (pls. 44–46)	15 (pls. 38–39)	21	24	15
27	28 (pl. 58)	29 (pl. 70)	27	37	23
28	29 (pls. 59–61)	30 (pls. 71–73)	28	38	24
23	23 (pls. 50–52, 58)	27 (pls. 62–66)	24	30	19
24	30 (pls. 62–63)	26 (pls. 58–61)	31	36	22
16	31 (pls. 64–67, 70)	31 (pls. 74–76)	30	34	27
D	24 (pl. 53)	23 (pl. 54)	22	29	26
26	32 (pls. 68–69)	28 (pls. 67–69)	32	35	28
30	34 (pls. 74, 76, 78)	34 (pls. 81–84)	35	40	25
29	33 (pls. 71–73)	33 (pls. 78–80)	37	42	29
31	35 (pls. 75, 77, 79)	35 (pls. 85–88)	36	41	31
pl. 39 (as contested)	36 (pl. 80)	—	33	39	—

Index of Collections

Paris, Musée du Louvre	*The Lacemaker* (Plate 31)
Paris, Private Collection	*Interior with an Astronomer* (Plate 26)
Rolin Collection	*A Lady at the Virginals* (Plate 36)
The Hague, Mauritshuis	*Diana and her Companions* (Plate 2)
	The View of Delft (Plate 5)
	Head of a Girl with a Pearl Earring (Plate 19)
Vienna, Kunsthistorisches Museum	*Interior with an Artist Painting a Model* (*The Artist's Studio* or *An Allegory of Painting*) (Plate 28)
Washington, National Gallery of Art	*Interior with a Lady Writing a Letter* (Plate 16)
	The Girl in a Red Hat (Plate 20)
	The Girl with a Flute (Plate 21)
	Interior with a Woman Weighing Gold (Plate 25)
Windsor Castle, Royal Collection	*Interior with a Lady at the Virginals with a Gentleman* (*The Music Lesson*) (Plate 14)